WHAT ORCHESTRA NEWCOMERS NEED TO KNOW

Lessons Learned from Thirty Years
Managing American Orchestras

Paul A. Helfrich

Copyright © 2025 Paul A. Helfrich

All rights reserved

No part of this book may be reproduced, or stored in a retrieval system, or transmitted in any form or by any means, electronic, mechanical, photocopying, recording, or otherwise, without express written permission of the author.

Paperback ISBN 979-8-218-64272-3

For Jessica, always my inspiration

CONTENTS

Title Page

Copyright

Dedication

Preface

1. The Four Main Constituencies of the Orchestra Organization — 1

2. Financial Reality Part 1: Ticket Sales Cover Less than Half the Costs — 13

3. Financial Reality Part 2: Orchestras' Costs Are Mostly Human and Always Growing — 17

4. Planning the Season — 22

5. How Do You Get into an Orchestra, Anyway? — 30

6. Concertgoing Conundrums — 35

7. Tis the Season — 43

8. The Modern Maestro: Changing Attitudes around the Conductor's Role — 47

9. The Evolving Role of the Executive Director — 52

10. Workers of the World Tune-Up: Labor Relations — 58

11. You Ought to Know — 65

12. Al Coda? Orchestras Confront the Future — 73

About The Author — 91

PREFACE

I must ruefully confess I still have anxiety dreams. These include the classic about realizing the final exam is today, but you never attended the class.

I have had some unique musical variants on this dream. I trained as a tubist, and in some of these dreams, I am in an orchestra playing tuba facing a lengthy complicated score I have never seen before. In others, I am holding an instrument I do not actually know how to play.

As I reflect on these writings, it occurs to me that there is a connection to orchestra management. I would opine that beginning a new job as an orchestra executive director is like being asked to play a complicated score you have heard about but never seen before, on an instrument that may not always be suited to the part.

My objective in these pages is to help explain that complicated score, and to assess how your "instrument" fits. I am thinking not just about new orchestra administrators, but new board members, volunteers, and musicians.

The field functions a lot on throwing organizational newcomers into the pool and then thinking – maybe – about swim lessons. I hope to provide a fast overview that will make joining an orchestra less intimidating, or even if you do not feel intimidated, to help assure that you are not merely experiencing the bliss of ignorance.

It is a field uniquely challenging but also uniquely rewarding. During my orchestra career, I had unforgettable great moments, and some I would not care to repeat. I hope you enjoy my thoughts and perspective.

Paul Helfrich
Raleigh, North Carolina
April 2025

1. THE FOUR MAIN CONSTITUENCIES OF THE ORCHESTRA ORGANIZATION

There is a Buddhist parable that is widely quoted, concerning a group of people who encounter an elephant on a pitch-dark night. Since they cannot see it, they each try to figure out what it is based on the parts they can feel.

One touches the trunk and concludes an elephant is a snake. Another touches a leg and decides an elephant must be like a tree. Another touches its side and imagines it to be a wall. Yet another touches a tusk and thinks it is a spear. They are all right, but also all wrong in concluding that the part of the elephant they have experienced most closely is the best representation of the whole.

I have thought of this parable often in my work with orchestras. Just like elephants are big, complicated animals, orchestras are big, complicated organizations with a variety of important parts and constituencies.

To most people, the musicians are the orchestra, end of story, and in terms of who plays the music, that is correct. But just as an airline requires mechanics, baggage handlers, gate agents, and flight attendants as well as pilots, the orchestra musicians have a supporting cast within the other three constituencies we will examine: board, staff, and non-board volunteers.

In healthy organizations, each is aware of the other and understands their contributions to the whole. In less healthy orchestras, there is a certain tunnel vision that sets in, in which various groups do not understand what the others do and why it is important. I will look at some of the most common pitfalls that can lead to such a situation.

The Board/Governance Volunteers

The Board of Directors, sometime referred to as Trustees, are the ultimate authority in the organization. Nonprofit organizations are required to have a Board, with details spelled out in their Articles of Incorporation and/or corporate Bylaws. The Board hires the top leadership - an Executive Director and a Music Director - and provides long-term and strategic direction for the organization. The Board also provides oversight from the community, to assure that the orchestra continues to serve its needs.

I like to think of the Board as having five key functions, divided between two broad groupings of "Governance" and "Advocacy:

Governance Functions

- Determine the strategic direction of the organization and make broad policy decisions (not day-to-day operating decisions).
- Approve and monitor an annual budget for the organization.
- Hire and fire the key staff members – Executive Director and Music Director.

Advocacy Functions

- Provide a voice for the community in the decision-making process of the orchestra, and a voice for the orchestra in the greater community.

- Raise money to support the organization in its nonprofit mission (typically sixty percent of an orchestra's budget comes from donations; the Board plays a critical leadership role in fundraising).

Unlike corporate boards in the for-profit sector, orchestra board members are uncompensated volunteers. These are typically community leaders in a variety of fields and very busy people. They are giving freely of their time, talents, and treasure (the other alliterative expression is "wealth, wisdom, and work") to help assure the orchestra's success. They get no remuneration or financial benefit whatsoever in exchange for their efforts. Instead, it costs THEM money; board members typically include some of the organization's most generous donors, and many orchestra boards have at least a suggested minimum annual gift. This is so important for others in the organization to understand.

Board members do not all have to have great musical knowledge, nor do all of them need to have detailed knowledge of accounting, management, or law. Since an orchestra board typically has twelve to forty-five members, there is room to recruit people with a variety of skills and backgrounds, so that there can be at least a few people with expertise in a variety of key areas.

They do all need a genuine belief, understanding, and respect for what the orchestra brings to the community, and an understanding of how non-profit organizations work.

It has become fashionable recently to say many orchestra boards are too large, and I agree that many governance decisions are better handled by a smaller group. However, the advocacy work of the Board is best served by a larger number, so that there can be broad representation from diverse segments of the community.

It is always a challenge for the Board's Nominating Committee, responsible for identifying and recruiting new Board members, to strike the balance between big donors, corporate representatives, persons with expertise in a variety of key areas, and inclusive representation of the community.

A valid criticism of ballet, opera, and orchestra boards is they have historically been largely white. This is no longer a sustainable model in cities that are now majority-minority, and most orchestras have made sincere efforts and good progress to diversify their boards. All this becomes much harder to do when the Board's membership is restricted to a smaller number.

I recommend a Board of twenty-four to thirty-six, organized into three "classes" of eight to twelve. A board member's term should be two to three years long, and they should be able to serve no more than three consecutive terms. The terms should be staggered so that a certain number of board members rotate off every year; in this way, there are always new voices coming into the organization's governance.

At their best, orchestra board members provide valuable expertise and perspective. They respect and value the work of professional musicians and support the work of the administrative staff without trying to interfere with it. They are generous donors and enthusiastic advocates in the community.

In less ideal situations, board members may not understand the unique world of musicians, their experience in the business sector may give them a negative disposition toward unions, and their business success may lead them to look down on persons who have chosen nonprofit work for a career. They may give far less than their capacity and think it is good enough. They may feel their role is to decide what color the season brochure should be, or to direct the day-to-day work of the staff, sometimes bypassing the Executive Director in the process.
Fortunately, there are many sources for non-profit training that can help board members, both old and new, understand their

vital role. It is also important for orchestras to have a robust orientation process specific to their own organization for their new directors, for they should never assume people come on to an orchestra board understanding how the organization works. That is the main reason I have written this book.

The Staff

The staff are the compensated administrative employees of the orchestra. They are typically organized into departments with areas of functional specialization, as follows:

- Administration/Finance – handles financial functions such as accounting, banking, and investing, as well as payroll, benefits, and other HR functions. This department plays a key role in the organization's accountability by tracking the numbers and keeping the board and management informed.
- Artistic Administration – only a separate department in larger orchestras; in smaller, it is usually part of either the Operations or the Executive office or, in part, of both. Artistic Administration has to do with the planning of special initiatives such as commissioning new works and organizing festivals, as well as the perennial work of booking guest soloists and planning repertoire. This department or function works very closely with the Music Director.
- Box Office – handles the direct sale of tickets to the public. This may be a large department, for orchestras that own and manage their own concert halls, or smaller, for orchestras that partner with a venue box office. It is also sometimes part of the marketing department, again mostly in smaller orchestras, rather than standing on its own. Whatever the structure, the box office plays a key role in customer relations and is often the department of first impressions.
- Development (often now called Philanthropy) –

"development" is short for "resource development," and this department is all about generating contributed resources, meaning it oversees fundraising. This includes keeping donor records and seeing that they are acknowledged, thanked, and receive proper receipts for tax purposes. Grant applications to government, foundation, and corporate funders come from this department, and it typically includes at least one skilled grant writer. It also, and most importantly, manages the orchestra's relationships with donors, both current and prospective. It is a truth of fundraising that people do not support causes, they support people, and they make the biggest gifts to people they know. That is why it is also critically important for this department to include people with superb people skills and a certain amount of charisma.

- Education – handles programs for learners of all ages, most importantly, school students. In days gone by, Education was often part of the Operations department, because educational work was seen first and foremost as a way to provide additional employment for musicians. Nowadays most orchestras have elevated their education department and view it more strategically, with a critical mission as part of the orchestra's service to the community for which the use of musicians is obviously necessary but no longer a raison d'être. Some education department titles may also include the words "community," "engagement," or "learning."
- Executive – the Board hires an Executive Director, sometimes called "President" or "President and CEO," to be the overall administrative director and all-around leader for the organization. All the other departments I am listing answer to the Executive Director, who is responsible for being coach, mentor, coordinator, and cheerleader. The Executive office is also generally in charge of the business of the Board, from sending meeting notices to making sure that accurate records and official minutes are kept.
- Library - orchestras handle thousands of sheets of printed music every season, and the Music Library has the crucial

responsibility to make sure the musicians have the right music at the right time. In all but the largest orchestras, the Music Library may be a sub-department of Operations. Similarly, in smaller orchestras, librarians are staff members and may be only part-time, but in big orchestras, they are full-time and members of the collective bargaining unit with union protections and work rules just like the musicians.

- Marketing – provides the motivation for people to buy tickets through advertising, media, and messaging. Orchestra marketing has evolved from old-fashioned "promotion" to a highly data-driven operation with very specific targeting of offers and messages, and is now also typically responsible for the orchestra's online activities, including website and social media. As noted, the box office may be a sub-department of marketing, and other sub-departments may include public/media relations and web content generation.
- Operations – manages the rehearsals and performances of the orchestra in all aspects, from scheduling venues months/years in advance to making sure the chairs and stands are set up correctly for every rehearsal. Most of the items governed by orchestra collective bargaining agreements (CBAs) depend on the Operations department to be properly fulfilled and enforced. Operations staff may need to coordinate with members of IATSE, the stagehands' union, if the orchestra performs in a "union hall," i.e., one where IATSE has jurisdiction and a collective bargaining agreement of their own.

Most orchestras put the bulk of their resources into direct mission fulfillment – performance and education programs – and that is as it should be. However, a downside of that is often that orchestra staff pay is much lower than might be found with comparable positions in the private sector, or even in more well-heeled non-profits like universities and hospitals. Benefits are also usually less. Board members and executives may have a tendency to expect staff members to do what they do strictly out of their love for the art form, in a way that takes advantage of those who truly do love music and will quickly drive away those whose connection with it is less central to their being.

In my experience, many orchestra staff members are tremendously talented, dedicated, hardworking, and resilient. They put in long hours including plenty of nights and weekends, as that is when orchestra performances tend to take place.

Staff members in less high-functioning organizations may begin to resent that the orchestra is not run for their convenience, and the schedule and hours, particularly during the main September-May season, are frequently a flash point – on top of the lower pay and benefits. They may resent the musicians for having fewer official hours on the clock, forgetting, or perhaps not being aware of, the many hours a musician must put in, away from the workplace, to be in top shape and prepared, to say nothing of the years of specialized training and study all professional musicians must have.

Keeping the staff happy, engaged, informed, and enthusiastic is one of the most important functions of the Executive Director. Board members can help her or him by supporting contemporary management styles and empathetic leadership, rather than buying into tired tropes of a "tough boss" to "keep the employees in line." There are times when that sort of skill is necessary, but in 2025, it cannot be an executive's first salient feature.

Direct Service Volunteers

"The League" – "The Guild" – "The Friends" – these are the direct service volunteers of an orchestra. "Direct service" means working alongside the staff in such functions as office and library volunteers. It often also includes work supporting the education department, which might be ushering at education concerts or giving docent presentations in schools. An historic function for direct service volunteers has also been to raise money for the orchestra through events such as balls, galas, fashion shows, golf tournaments, and other similar activities.

Direct service volunteers are separate from the Board, although they usually have representation on the Board, and they have none of the Board's governance authority. Most of them are doing what they do out of their love for the orchestra and its programs, and a desire for meaningful volunteer experiences that let them feel close to those things.

In earlier times, many orchestra volunteer organizations began as "women's associations," because the boards would be made up of male executives with only a few women members, usually quite wealthy ones. Times have changed and volunteer associations now always include men and women, just as boards do, although some volunteer groups are still largely female. That is a real challenge going forward, because the activities I describe above require a large commitment of time and work – especially organizing fundraising events. Newer generations may be less inclined or less able to make such commitments of time. Further, they may also prefer to work on different projects, over time, for different causes, rather than devoting themselves to an orchestra as their primary cause. For these reasons, many orchestra volunteer organizations now encounter some level of difficulty recruiting new members, and even more so recruiting members to take on leadership roles.

I have met so many wonderful people in volunteer associations – often some of the orchestra's most enthusiastic fans and boosters. They are the people the orchestra may count on through thick and thin. With that said, there are several ways volunteer groups can start to go off track. They may resent the staff, which usually manifests as, "They're getting paid, I'm not; therefore they should do everything I expect them to do, when I want them to do it—no excuses." Since they often organize their own fundraising events, there may be clashes or conflicts with the orchestra's Development staff, often manifesting as fighting over sponsors.

They may resent the Board if they feel the Board is not sufficiently supportive or appreciative of their efforts. Like bad-behaving board members, they may resent musicians, which usually manifests as, "What do you mean they won't play for free – don't they know we're volunteers?" Further, going back to older times, volunteer organizations may be associated with a certain social set that will give the orchestra an elitist appearance. A tendency to hold events at country clubs has not helped in this regard.
With all the challenges of changing times and demographics before them, many volunteer associations are now proactively thinking of how best to reinvent themselves for the years to come. This will take different forms in different communities, but just as with other traditional volunteer groups, like service clubs, change of some sort is inevitable.

The Musicians

The musicians are the compensated artistic employees of the organization and, most importantly, the reason for its existence, for there is no live orchestral music without real live musicians to play it.

Most orchestras started in two ways. Most often, a group of prominent citizens decided their community needed an orchestra and formed the nucleus of a board. As part of their organizational efforts, they would recruit musicians as a key first step. Other orchestras were started by the musicians themselves who, to fund and support their efforts, began to recruit community leaders as a board as one of their own first steps.

In either scenario, musicians are central - the most necessary thing for an orchestra to fulfill its mission. Once an orchestra becomes more active, a staff is needed to organize and support its efforts beyond what a board or other volunteers may be able or willing to do. It should be abundantly clear, though, that the other groups exist to support and enable the work of the musicians. In my work as an Executive Director, I would often thank patrons "for their support of great music and the musicians who play it," as a subtle way of reminding them you cannot have one without the other.

Musicians become members of orchestras through demanding audition, probation, and tenure processes. As with staff members, compensation and benefits may not compare favorably to other fields, and that can be especially galling for musicians. Why? Given their years of highly specialized training and nurturing of individual of talents, to say nothing of their investments in expensive instruments and accessories, many musicians – correctly – view themselves as akin to other top professionals like doctors and lawyers, but with compensation (even in the largest orchestras) lagging behind what such other professionals command. Many develop a certain chip on their shoulders regarding all things having to do with compensation, as a result.

Many also become so focused on their needs that they have unrealistic expectations of staff, expecting them to control the weather or people and circumstances who do not report to the staff. Musicians may not understand that their governing board are uncompensated volunteers. They may not understand just how orchestras are paid for, with tickets only covering about 40% of the expenses. When sixty cents of every dollar you are paid comes from contributions, that is a very different set of business realities compared to one where 100% of every dollar comes from selling iPhones or automobiles.

After 30 years as an orchestra executive director, I learned never to assume that one part of the organization understands what the others do, or why, or how. That is why leadership is so important. Scheduled formal activities like orientations can help, but it is unrealistic to expect everyone to be on the same page all the time, regardless of how many orientations or information-sharing sessions may be held. With all this in mind, an orchestra leader must serve each day as the hub at the center of the wheel, keeping all the other parts informed and aware of what the others are doing, and fostering respect and appreciation all around.

Orchestras attract many talented and dedicated people. When they are all pointed in the same direction, the results can be amazing. My time with orchestras connected me with some of the finest people I have ever met, and they included members of all the four constituencies I discussed above – board members with tremendous wisdom and perspective, as well as generosity; volunteers who were so dedicated; staff members so driven and hardworking; musicians with such amazing artistry.

Prominent consultant and author Joan Garry says, "Non-profits are messy," and orchestras are the messiest. They are big and complicated, with lots of voices and competing perspectives. Running one is not easy, not for the faint of heart, but also an opportunity to serve something of true value. That is orchestra management in a nutshell.

2. FINANCIAL REALITY PART 1: TICKET SALES COVER LESS THAN HALF THE COSTS

Orchestras are not-for-profit organizations dependent on contributions, but the extent to which this is true is often masked to people outside the field, by the fact that we do charge admission and sell tickets to most concerts. While orchestras always make a big deal out of the free concerts they offer, the reality is most public orchestral events carry an admission charge.

Orchestras sell two types of tickets – season tickets or subscriptions, meaning a package of tickets sold, usually at a discount, to a whole series of events – and single tickets, which are admissions to individual events, one at a time. A person who holds a season ticket is called a subscriber.

Season subscribers have always been of critical importance to American orchestras. These are the people who have committed in advance to an entire series of concerts. They provide an assurance that typically over half the seats are sold before the season begins. This is key to the ability of orchestras to plan a full season of diverse repertoire in advance and to take some risks with less familiar artists and programming.

One of the great texts of arts management is Danny Newman's Subscribe Now!: Building Arts Audiences through Dynamic Subscription Promotion, published in 1977 and very much still worth reading. Mr. Newman describes a labor-intensive process for selling as many subscriptions as possible with evangelical zeal.

As lifestyles and habits have changed - more two-career couples, persons starting families later, increased competition from all sorts of new media – the subscription model has faced increasing pressure. It is a very different world compared to the 1970s. The COVID-19 pandemic further accelerated a decline in subscription sales. Recovery has been slow – the best most orchestras can say is now some variant of, "We are almost back to ninety percent of our pre-pandemic level."

When subscriptions decline, orchestras become more and more reliant on single tickets, which are more expensive to sell; unlike subscriptions, which might be sold on the strength of one brochure and renewal mailing, single tickets take constant advertising and promotion, in a whole variety of media, for sales goals to be met.

With that said, many folks are still surprised to learn that all ticket sales – even if we crush every single goal in the budget – do not cover the costs of most concerts. That is because each concert an orchestra presents requires its own set of rehearsals and other associated expenses, including marketing, hall rental, guest artists, and stagehands.

Classics Series concerts, often called Masterworks concerts by other orchestras, are the most expensive of all, because they require the greatest number of musicians and the most rehearsal time. At best, ticket sales will cover about half the cost of a Classics Series concert, and overall, ticket sales cover only about forty percent of an orchestra's projected expenses every year. Your mileage may vary, but forty percent is the most accurate generalization that may be made.

This is where I find many new board members who look perplexed. "You mean you sell tickets and still lose money? What kind of a business model is that?"

This is a point that is critically important, both to understanding the purpose of orchestras and the process they use to get there. The purpose is to serve the community with cultural and educational events – not to make a profit for shareholders. The process, further, emphasizes artistic quality and gainful employment for artists, similarly over making a profit.

It does not make money, but this business model allows an orchestra to be in the community 365 days a year and to perform hundreds of concerts, typically including many for schoolchildren. How could we make it profitable? If one orchestra could perfect one program and never have to rehearse again and then tour all over the country playing that program, night after night, that might be profitable. That is the touring Broadway show model. By contrast, the 365-days-a-year model of an organization that is resident in and responsive to a community allows a much greater depth and breadth of service and a greater impact on lives.

Orchestras must still pay the bills, and that is where philanthropy comes in. The other sixty percent of the income is contributed. We depend on the generosity of individuals, corporations, foundations, and other funders that share our vision and want the transformative power of live music in their community.

That is the financial reality of a symphony orchestra. Tickets do not pay for even half of it. We recognize that we must maintain a reasonable range of ticket prices to be accessible to many – if we were to amortize our expenses over the capacity of our halls and charge what it "really" costs, every ticket would be two hundred dollars or more. That means we depend on generous funders to help make up the difference and keep the music alive.

You will not be in the field long before you realize that funders do not give automatically. In my experience, they look for a compelling vision, a commitment to excellence, and a willingness to keep pushing the envelope. Orchestras thus face a constant balancing act between the pragmatic and the aspirational, what we can afford versus where we need to go, the value of our people versus our obligation to keep the orchestra in good financial shape. It is never easy.

3. FINANCIAL REALITY PART 2: ORCHESTRAS' COSTS ARE MOSTLY HUMAN AND ALWAYS GROWING

As I just discussed, one important financial reality of orchestras is that ticket sales usually pay less than half of total expenses and we therefore depend on the philanthropy of generous donors to make up the difference.

An equally important thing is that most of the costs of orchestras are human costs, beginning with the sixty to seventy musicians you see on stage at each concert. They are joined by conductors and guest artists and supported backstage by stagehands and technical personnel. Staff run the business, handling logistics, scheduling, finance, personnel, music library, marketing, program development and philanthropy. Because orchestras always employ a lot of substitutes and extra musicians in addition to their core musicians, they pay many in the course of a year.

At the Orlando Philharmonic, my last orchestra, we would typically have more than three hundred W-2 forms (employees) and over one hundred 1099 forms (contractors) to send out each January.

Human costs mean payroll, and people have a reasonable expectation to be paid more over time, for as we all know, costs for all goods and services increase over time, including daily staples like food, fuel, and clothing. Orchestras thus always see their costs increasing from year to year, in almost every category within the budget.

That is the pressure on the expense side. Meanwhile, on the revenue side, ticket purchasers are sensitive to price increases, and most donors do not make automatic increases for inflation. In my experience, most people who give $1,000 think, correctly, that they are making a generous gift, and keep it the same from year to year. Keeping pace with our costs would, over time, be more like $1,000, then $1,050, then $1,103, etc. While most donors do not do that, occasionally some do make a major leap in giving, like going from $5,000 to $10,000, and it is always cause for celebration – and appreciation – when that happens.

As a rule, though, increasing philanthropic income means finding more donors, and that takes more staff resources, and the result is a constant battle for revenue to keep up with expenses. For the reasons mentioned above, revenue tends to be static or inelastic, whereas expenses are dynamic and always growing.

In the last chapter I mentioned Danny Newman's Subscribe Now!. An equally important text in the arts administration field is "Performing Arts – The Economic Dilemma," a 1966 study (almost always characterized as a "landmark" study) by William J. Baumol and William G. Bowen, subtitled "A Study of Problems Common to Theater, Opera, Music and Dance." In this study, Baumol and Bowen, both professors of economics at Princeton University, lay out the same issues I have described above, often referred to as "the income gap."

The arts are labor-intensive by nature. It takes the same number of people to play Beethoven's Fifth now as it did in the nineteenth century. Technology has not made the production process more efficient. Any labor-intensive field that cannot take full advantage of technological efficiencies such as automation can expect its costs to rise faster than the rate of inflation; it will not be able to pay for itself and will rely on contributions, but unless there is an exponential increase in sources of contributed income, one may expect deficits of increasing size.

It is not anyone's fault - not greedy unions, not lazy management, not the decline of music education – it is endemic to the system as it is constructed. One may therefore expect arts organizations to generally be in a state of controlled crisis, with some crises from time to time spiraling out of control.

While the issue has been well-documented by Princeton professors, no less, for over half a century, most people in the field act as if these facts do not exist. Again, no one is at fault; my general premise for this writing is that most people come into the field, whether as staff, managers, musicians, or board members, without really knowing what they are getting into. Without question, though, there is a certain willful denial as well; as Upton Sinclair said, "It is difficult to get a man to understand something when his salary depends on his not understanding it."

Board members often, with good intentions, think they might be able to solve this issue single-handedly. Unless that hand is reaching for a very large wallet, it is unlikely to be so, but one area that often attracts a lot of board interest is ticket sales.

Even if it is less than half of the budget, ticket revenue is still important, and it is a fact that some concerts do sell better than others. It is not too hard to predict what those will be. In the opera world, it is A-B-C: Aida, La Boheme, and Carmen. In ballet, it is The Nutcracker, Swan Lake, and then basically everything else. For orchestras, Beethoven's 9th, Carmina Burana, the Mozart & Verdi Requiems, the Rachmaninoff Piano Concertos, pretty much anything by Tchaikovsky especially the Piano and Violin Concertos and some big showcase pieces like Mussorgsky's "Pictures at an Exhibition" – these are the things we know will fill the seats, or at least more than an all-Lutoslawski program will. On the pops side of things, we know that holiday concerts, Broadway, movies, and well-known guest artists always sell well.

Classical concerts that sell well still lose money, but less than those that do not sell many tickets, and some pops concerts actually make money. In the pre-pandemic world, I could count on my "Rockin' Orchestra" series concerts with the Dayton Philharmonic to add $15,000 to the bottom line, on average, for each one we did.
So inevitably, once more fiscally attuned board members become aware of this, the question gets asked, "Why don't we just do more of the things that make money, and less of the things that don't?"

It is a good question, so let's look at several constituencies that benefit from a broad range of programming, and the importance of such programming to an orchestra's mission.

Our audiences appreciate variety in repertoire, not Beethoven's Ninth and the Tchaikovsky Violin Concerto every single season. This is particularly true of subscription audiences. Musicians similarly expect to play a broad range of music, not just a narrow slice of popular works. Orchestral musicians have a different mindset than Broadway performers who may sing the same show, repeatedly, eight shows a week for years. (As an aside, I frequently wished that they did not, but the profession is littered with the remains of managers who thought they were going to change how musicians think.)

Contributors are often motivated specifically by certain works and artists. Individual donors are often enamored of celebrity artists; just as they drive expensive cars, big donors often like to support appearances by expensive artists with a greater degree of name recognition. On the other hand, foundation funders may have a particular interest in new and diverse repertoire, perversely, the very thing that is less likely to sell tickets. While they may have different interests, we depend on contributed income to a greater degree than ticket sales, so aligning with our various funders' interests is important.

In my view, while one can program pops with a primary goal of maximizing revenue, that approach cannot be followed in the same way with core repertoire programming, the so-called "Classics" or "Masterworks" concerts.

Our mission is to serve the community and to advance the art form. We will always come back regularly to Rachmaninoff's 3rd, Beethoven's 5th, and other favorites, but we should do it as part of a balanced and varied approach to programming that recognizes some responsibility to new repertoire – just as museums make a commitment to artists living today, as well as to those who came before.
In the next chapter, I will examine the programming process in greater detail.

4. PLANNING THE SEASON

In the late winter to early spring of every year, orchestras announce their upcoming seasons, to begin the following September. Thus, even as we are in the final months of the current season, orchestras are rolling out their programming for the next one. That is a year and a half in advance for some of those programs.

Why so much notice? It is because of the subscription ticket model I described in chapter two, one that remains the centerpiece of most orchestras' earned revenue efforts. If one was to go back forty to fifty years, you would find many orchestras generated more than eighty percent of their ticket revenue from subscriptions.

Now, it is much less, for many reasons mentioned earlier – busier lifestyles, two-career families, that ever-growing competition for leisure time. While orchestras now must depend far more heavily on individual concert revenue, even so, season subscriptions and the annual campaign to sell them remain critically important.

It is not just a big chunk of revenue, it is the timing of it, in advance of the programs in question, which means that in good years there is money in the bank going into the next season, and in less good years there is an influx of cash in the middle of the current season, a time of high expenses. This is often helpful as an orchestra waits for big grants to be paid out and recalcitrant donors to open their wallets.

Further, your subscribers are a large group of people who have demonstrated a special commitment to your orchestra, by deciding on – and paying for – their participation well in advance. These are typically the most enthusiastic patrons, and it is helpful to always keep them excited about what is on the horizon. Announcing a full season months in advance helps to keep their interest.

Most people do not realize, when you get that shiny new brochure in the mail or see the announcement in your social media, it is the culmination of over a year of planning. There is quite a bit that happens to get to that point, a procedure I worked through over thirty times with four different orchestras.

As a first step, at least eighteen/perhaps twenty-four months in advance of a given season's start, an orchestra's internal management team agrees on proposed concert dates, aligns them with the Music Director's schedule, and shares them for planning purposes with regular partners, like opera or ballet companies for whom the orchestra plays. Inevitably there will be conflicts with other events in a community with a thriving arts scene, so priority is given to avoiding them with the orchestra's most regular collaborators.

Some orchestras own or control their own concert halls; many others work with a venue under separate management. If that is the case, then very early in the process, the orchestra will attempt to get those dates locked in at the venue.

Many venues do not want to commit to giving the orchestra its requested dates when the orchestra asks for them, because they are hoping to book Broadway shows or other lucrative attractions they may not know about yet. In general, Broadway and commercial music does not plan as far in advance as does the classical world. This can create a significant challenge, because an orchestra manager cannot sign a contract with a guest artist for a certain date unless they know they have secured a venue for that date. It is also wise not to put a date on a schedule for professional musicians without that same level of certainty, because musician union contracts are typically restrictive of schedule changes. Further, one cannot begin selling tickets to dates of which one is not sure.

Many venues have an understanding that they were built with the needs of the local symphony, opera, or ballet in mind, and take a collaborative approach to scheduling. Others can be more adversarial; this can add considerably to an orchestra executive's already high stress level.

At some point, the orchestra will have confidence in its dates, and at that point, the Music Director and Artistic Planning team usually focus first on their flagship Classical or Masterworks series. They will want to identify the season's "tent poles" – these could be a major piece of repertoire, or a unique guest artist, or combinations of both.

The Music Director is typically most involved with the Classical series and others where they do the lion's share of conducting. Music Directors may have little or nothing to do with the planning of Pops, Education, Film-With-Orchestra, Rock Tribute, or other special concerts, which may be handled more at the staff level. It varies depending on the size and staffing level of the orchestra; small orchestra Music Directors tend to have a greater overall responsibility for planning, while in big orchestras it is shared among many players.

Whatever the planning team may be, they will work through multiple iterations of ideas for all their various series, including repertoire and soloists. In many cases, the first people to see and review these plans are members of an Artistic Advisory Committee, including both Board members, staff, and musicians.

These can be lively meetings, as each constituency has its own agenda within the larger scheme of things. Marketing staff want programs they can sell (and they are not the only ones!). Musicians want to play interesting and varied repertoire. Conductors have their pet projects and bucket list pieces. Development staff want programs that will appeal to their big donors, and board members on the committee may strongly advocate for their own repertoire ideas.

To make all this work, it is important to frame the committee's mission as one of "advise and consent." The onus is on the Music Director and staff to generate ideas. The committee does not do their job for them but rather helps to vet ideas and provide initial feedback. With that said, politically savvy Music Directors (and managers) will listen carefully when this committee meets and make sure to implement at least a few of the ideas that come up. Managers have an interest in all constituencies feeling like they are heard, so that no one becomes alienated.

Major classical soloists and conductors tend to have their seasons planned one to two years in advance, so orchestras must start early to have a chance of getting the artists they want. Pops acts usually work with a shorter time frame, but since seasons are announced as a whole, including all the various series, planning for those other series is usually on the same eighteen to twenty-four months out schedule as the classical programming.

By nine months prior to the start of the given season, there needs to be a fully fleshed-out plan with guest artists and programs. This information in basic form is then turned over to the staff marketing team to be packaged for the customer, including such tasks as descriptive copywriting, graphic design, and collection of photographic imagery to support the new season. At the same time, the orchestra's Box Office/Ticketing team will begin the season "build" in whatever ticketing software the orchestra may use. This involves setting up each event for sale with the correct seating zones and pricing and building subscription packages for the subscribers. Hard copy renewal materials will also be developed for subscribers, to support the season announcement. The idea is always to make the renewal process as smooth and easy as possible, while still allowing patrons the opportunity to request changes in seating or series.

By February or March, orchestras are finally ready to make that exciting announcement for the season that will open the following September.

I have always found this process to be one of the most interesting and important parts of orchestra management. It is a process of taking a lot of "maybes" and "what-ifs," building a rich and diverse season, and getting it ready to be promoted to the public. It is one of the best ways orchestras can attract attention to themselves. Excitement around future programming can be a great catalyst for contributed support; as industry expert Michael Kaiser has consistently advocated, orchestras that can share privately that they have exciting plans even further into the future, not just for the next season, will have an easier time fostering interest and investment from donors.

That is the mechanics of the process but let us get back to the decision-making; how the choices for programming are made. It is not easy, as orchestras are trying to cover many bases and serve many masters. They are trying to keep the subscribers happy, and usually this means familiar favorite works and well-known soloists. They are usually trying to do at least something to keep the repertoire growing, not static; this means including less familiar repertoire and works by living composers. Most orchestras of any stature regularly commission new works and participate in commissioning consortiums with other groups. Orchestras also try to provide opportunities for up-and-coming soloists as well as those with an established career.

Orchestras are also now trying to correct a long legacy of exclusion from the repertoire, specially of works by women and people of color, works that are worthy of a place on concert programs but are only now getting that chance.

If an orchestra has fewer than a dozen Classical series concerts in which to do all this, it can be quite a challenge. I never got to plan a twenty-four concert flagship series, but I am sure that those who do will say it is not any easier for them.

As Lincoln said, you cannot please all the people all the time. Nevertheless, all Music and Executive Directors should be able to make a compelling case for how each season has addressed the needs and interests of many different constituencies, and how each season contains something new and innovative, not just "what we've always done."

I am fascinated by how changes in taste and artistic judgment have affected orchestra programming over the years. Decades ago, orchestras played more Baroque music in big-orchestra arrangements. The rise of the Early Music movement and period practice put an end to that, although the popularity of certain Baroque pieces like Vivaldi's *Four Seasons* and Handel's *Messiah* mean that orchestras continue to play them using smaller forces and whatever the latest understanding of "authentic" style may be.

Covering so many bases can lead to certain composers and eras getting skipped over. I am always happy to see an orchestra programming the symphonies of Schubert, Mendelssohn, and Schumann, rather than skipping directly from Beethoven to Brahms and Tchaikovsky. I also agree with one of our fields' great leaders, Henry Fogel, that a lot of "lighter" classical works – for example, works of the Strauss family, or the entire catalogue of Franz von Suppé – became unfairly consigned to pops and outdoor programs. There is a lot of great music in this category that is now making its way back onto main subscription series programs. We must note, though, that orchestra seasons are not the internet – they do not have unlimited space for everything. Playing a full range of music of established repertoire can lead to less time for new music. Playing more new music can leave less time for neglected works of the past. Bringing in historically excluded composers can create the impression of less attention to acknowledged masterworks. It is always a struggle to balance these competing needs and priorities.

While many in the field would consider this to be sacrilege, I think future audiences will be less interested in the distinctions we make so much of between "classical" and "pops", between concert works and film scores, between art music and popular songs. They may wonder why they cannot hear film music of John Williams on the same program with a great symphony, or a Taylor Swift concert suite on a program with song suites of the past. As time goes by, I think combinations like that will become more common.

After all, what does "pops" really mean? It is not really the "popular" music of the exact moment, but always music that was popular at some time, typically music that will correspond to the youthful times of an earlier generation. Just as older concertgoers respond well to classic Broadway and Great American Songbook, baby boomers respond well to classic rock and Motown, GenXers to the Indigo Girls and REM, and so forth. It means many things to many people, and as time goes by, it will be increasingly hard to define.

It is also unwise for orchestras to define what they do on their main series as "art music" and everything else as "entertainment." That is another distinction that will become increasingly difficult to make, and if "art" becomes synonymous with "rarefied, exclusive, and remote" it will not be a good development for orchestras, as they are organizations that can thrive only with the broad support of a community including philanthropists who are convinced of their benefits.

There will be vigorous debate, experimentation, failure, and success as we sort through this. I was always happier talking about programming than about the budget, and I look forward to this journey.

5. HOW DO YOU GET INTO AN ORCHESTRA, ANYWAY?

Most people are aware that artists become members of professional companies, like ballets, operas, and symphonies, by audition, but most people also have no idea what that entails. Hollywood has not helped; I am sure many feel a company or ensemble audition is like the climactic scene of Flashdance (1983), in which a raw young talent wins over bored skeptics with a performance developed entirely on her own.
https://www.youtube.com/watch?v=dsCl2kXJca4

Others may think of Emma Stone's audition scene in La La Land (2016), also presented as an entirely improvised exercise: "Tell us a story...you're a storyteller." https://www.youtube.com/watch?v=NlIVb0DgmLA

Once again, natural talent blazes forth in an unmistakable manner. Of course, she gets the part – how could it be otherwise?

As any orchestral musician will tell you, the reality of orchestral auditions is far different. There is no improvisation: a long list of orchestral excerpts, any one of which may be called for during the audition, must be painstakingly prepared in advance. Auditionees may get to choose from some possible solo works, but almost always they are standard repertoire; you cannot come in with your own thing.

Above all, those orchestral excerpts must be polished till they shine. They must be perfectly in tune, perfectly in rhythm, with just the right amount of expression. Too much may be deemed idiosyncratic. Too little may be deemed robotic. Audition committees are looking for candidates who can do certain things in a certain way – in this case, flawlessly.

The training to do this does not just happen, nor can it be self-taught. It is not a matter of natural talent alone, rather it is a matter of natural talent honed through years of diligent preparation, including private lessons, youth orchestras, summer camps and festivals, and of course conservatory training at the collegiate and graduate school level. And as the old joke about the way to Carnegie Hall goes, practice, practice, practice, for hours a day. All that training has a cost – increasingly fine instruments, private teachers, youth orchestra tuition, summer camps and festivals, travel to the same – it all costs money. Scholarships never cover everything – for instance, a tuition scholarship to a youth orchestra still leaves, for many, the problem of getting there physically, to rehearsals and performances that may be miles and miles from the home.

Honing one's skills to the point where one is ready for a highly competitive audition takes all of that, over years of preparation, and just being ready is no guarantee of a positive result. There are very few positions open at any given time, relative to the supply of interested musicians. There may be dozens and dozens of candidates auditioning for a single position, and the standards are so high, sometimes dozens and dozens of candidates are heard and still no one is deemed acceptable.

Orchestras go to great lengths to make sure the process is fair and free from bias. Compared to typical job interviews, where resumes are shared with an interviewer who is seeing candidates with their own eyes, orchestra auditions are "blind," meaning conducted behind a screen, and the committees that make hiring decisions do not know to whom they are listening, including their gender or ethnicity.

They do not see resumes during the audition, and great steps are taken to make sure there is no way of identifying anything about a given candidate, for instance by providing a carpeted walkway so that the difference in sound between heels and flat shoes cannot be noted as auditionees walk in. Orchestras have also begun taking steps to counter potential abuses of technology; committee members may be asked to turn in their cell phones during the audition, to assure that no shenanigans are going on via text message or e-mail.

Overall, winning a competitive, nationally advertised audition is the only way to become a member of a professional orchestra in this country, and it is a difficult and demanding process.

That is how the musicians you see on stage at an orchestra concert got there. This unique system has many pros and cons, and while it would be hard to find someone who really likes the process as it currently exists, we have yet to produce a suitable alternative. As Churchill said of democracy, it is the worst system possible, except for all the others that have been tried.

Even a musician who has accomplished the impressive feat of winning a competitive audition is not out from under the microscope yet, for new orchestral musicians spend at least one year, maybe two, on probation. This is essentially an evaluation period during which the Music Director (alone, in some cases, as part of a committee or advised by a committee, in others) determines if the audition did, in fact, select the right candidate, and that the winner should remain part of the orchestra.

If the answer is yes, and a candidate is determined to have passed their probationary period, they receive tenure. Much like tenured university faculty, tenure means their ongoing employment from season to season is now guaranteed. There are processes through which a tenured musician may be removed, but they are complex and lengthy, and considerably more difficult than letting go of a probationary musician. That is not easy, either, which may explain the occasional "no-hire" audition. If a committee is not sure, they may prefer not to hire rather than rely on the probationary process to affirm or disprove their decision, as it becomes a considerably more personal matter once someone has begun playing in an orchestra.

Another feature of orchestral tenure is the right, after a certain number of years of service, to request a leave of absence. This is also somewhat analogous to academic tenure, which generally includes the right, at some point, to a sabbatical leave. Musicians take leaves of absence from their positions for all sorts of reasons, including to be on probation in another orchestra after winning an audition. In this way, a musician may see if they get tenure in a new situation, while knowing that their old position will still be held for them for the duration of their leave.

The field's recent focus on improving diversity has brought some overdue attention to the tenure process. In an academic setting, a "tenure-track" professor must demonstrate excellence in teaching and especially research, documented through published work in scholarly journals. They usually put together a dossier of their work and submit it for review to a committee of their peers and to their dean or department head. In theory, a professor who has had papers published and who demonstrates a strong track record in teaching and service to the university through such activities as serving on committees will receive tenure. In practice, as in all human endeavors, politics can play a role. Saying the wrong thing to the wrong person at a cocktail party can have unfortunate consequences, as anyone who has spent time in or around academia can attest.

Tenure criteria in a symphony orchestra are far more nebulous than in the academic world. There is no requirement to publish, and someone who plays well enough to win a highly competitive audition is unlikely to get into an orchestra and have difficulty playing at a high level. What may be a pitfall, however, is something generally described as "fitting in." This may have a legitimate artistic dimension, such as being unwilling to match an established sound or style of playing within a section. However, it may also extend to personality issues and, just as in academia, to getting on the wrong side of the wrong people. Orchestras are full of strongly opinionated, ego-driven individuals, as one would expect in any competitive and demanding field. We have all heard the adage about how power corrupts, and without question, there are persons in the orchestra world who will use power – including power over peers in the tenure process – in an arbitrary and capricious manner.

This is a particular challenge when people win membership in an orchestra from constituencies historically not well-represented in the field. While orchestras are now roughly 50% female, this is still not the case in brass sections, and women continue to encounter difficulties, in some orchestras, with "fitting in," sometimes reflected in difficulty gaining tenure. There have also been well-publicized cases around the tenure process involving musicians of color. In my opinion, this is an area where a greater degree of administration and even board oversight would be beneficial.

All musicians can do what they do only with our enthusiastic participation, beginning with our presence in the audience. I have tremendous respect for all musicians who have dedicated themselves to their art, which is in many ways a calling as well as a profession. They need and deserve our respect, our admiration, and our support.

6. CONCERTGOING CONUNDRUMS

Here are some of the toughest conundrums facing orchestras: outside, of course, of the perennial financial challenges laid out in the first two chapters. These are some of the hot-button topics that orchestra managers are often asked about, and they are not easy to answer!

Dress – Audiences

"What should I wear?" This is one of the questions most frequently asked of orchestra and box office staff. It reflects the unfortunate stereotype of orchestras being only for the wealthy and elite – there are literally folks that imagine that they must wear a tuxedo or ball gown, just to attend a concert! When asked this question, orchestra staff generally go to such great lengths not to offend anyone or play into the stereotype that they may say, "Just dress as you feel comfortable." It's well-meant, but for many, still doesn't provide enough information. I prefer, "Dress as you would if you were going to a restaurant where a server will take your order." Whatever that means to you, it will work.

Here is the problem. While orchestra staff and musicians do not especially care what audience members wear, as long as it fits within the cliché of "no shoes, no shirt, no service" – we just want to fill the seats, for heaven's sake – others in the audience may be considerably more judgmental.

I grew up in an era when even men who worked outdoors in rough work clothes all week long would don a jacket and tie to go to church on Sunday. Those days are long gone. There are fewer and fewer occasions where people dress up once they get past the high school prom. However, there are still many in symphony audiences who believe their fellow attendees should be dressed for a formal occasion.

In my opinion, this is one of the worst things that anyone who cares about the future of the art form can do: sneer at people who attend concerts in T-shirts, sandals, ripped jeans or whatever they may deem inappropriate. If we make people feel excluded, those concert halls are just going to get less and less full.

Further, while there is at least something of an artistic argument to be made about some of the other topics I will examine, like clapping between movements, it really should not affect your appreciation of the music if the person down the row from you has chosen to wear shorts. Dress-shaming needs to stop.

Dress – Musicians

One of my personal pet peeves is that orchestra men are asked to dress like a liveried servant from the Edwardian era, like they're going to dinner at the Captain's Table on the RMS Titanic. Most men no longer wear such formal attire as white tie and tails even to be married, or to be buried, two places where it might have been more common in the past.

Orchestra women, on the other hand, are essentially told to dress like Morticia Addams – "Wear black." The result is often some of the dullest outfits one will ever see, and even worse, frequently a poor match for the extreme formality of the men's dress.

It is true that many orchestra patrons still prefer this "traditional" look, but here one must try to adopt the perspective of someone seeing it for the first time. Now that we are well into the 21st century, how does it look? No one dresses like that other than orchestra musicians.

I think orchestras have emphasized uniformity and tradition to a fault. I think masculine dress (how most orchestras now define it, rather than "men" or "women") should probably include a jacket, and yes, the color black may be involved in some way. But for feminine dress, I would like to see those frumpy concert black outfits gone for good. I think the feminine dress should be elegant, and formal, and allow for some individuality. I approve of bright colors or black, as well as sequins, shiny jewelry, sleeveless, plunging necklines, all typically forbidden in orchestra collective bargaining agreements. Those sorts of individual style choices should not be required, but they should not be forbidden, either.

I fear that many orchestras will try to change from the past with uniform outfits that will make musicians appear to be oddly formal flight attendants. In my view, musicians should dress like people doing something fun and exciting, and too much uniformity can be a problem. After all, it is not sports, where one must be able to tell one team from another!

Clapping Between Movements

The practice of not clapping between movements of a multi-movement work is typically viewed as "correct" practice by more experienced audience members. Newcomers, on the other hand, may have never encountered such a thing before, and anxiety about "when to clap" can be off-putting and discourage future attendance.

In fact, the practice of applauding only after the final movement is a relatively recent development in the history of Western art music. It only caught on toward the end of the 19th century – in Mozart's day, it was the norm and even a mark of cultural sophistication to not only clap, but to talk during a performance! Only novices who had never heard an orchestra before sat in silence. While I am not suggesting we return to those practices, it is important to keep in mind that our current norms did not come down on stone tablets from above.

What makes it especially challenging is that there are situations where applauding between movements makes perfect sense, others where it does not, and others where opinions vary.

Examples of movements where applauding after feels right and silence seems weird: first movements of Tchaikovsky's Piano Concerto No. 1 and Violin Concerto; first movement of Beethoven's Violin Concerto.

Examples of movements where applauding after feels wrong and breaks the mood: second movement of Beethoven's "Eroica" Symphony; any slow movement in a Mahler symphony; probably anything marked "funebre."

Tricky ones: the third movement of Tchaikovsky's "Pathétique" Symphony practically screams for applause, because it sounds like a finale. If silence is observed, however, it gives the drastic change of mood at the start of the fourth movement much more impact. I also feel that applauding after a Scherzo movement is fine if the work goes on to an upbeat final movement (Beethoven's Seventh), but less so if next up is a contemplative adagio (Schumann's Second).

It is hard to generalize. Telling people to count the movements as they go by often does not work, as many pieces have "attacca" movements that flow into the next one without pause. Telling people to wait till others around them start to applaud can feel patronizing and contribute to a feeling of not fitting in.

However, it is a fact that silence is an important part of music, and the feeling a composer has tried to create can sometimes be disrupted by premature applause.

My feeling is this can only be managed in one of two ways: we just let applause happen, and if it is at a time that feels right, the conductor should have the orchestra stand and acknowledge it. If not, they should wait for it to be over but not acknowledge it at all; no quick turning around and flashing a pained grimace. But perhaps the best way of all to manage it would be to have conductors carefully and kindly explain their preferences at the beginning of each multi-movement work. That can include saying when it is OK (big first movements of concertos) and when they want to discourage it (after profound adagios). It is not enough to just put it in the program notes; not everyone reads them—or to mention it in pre-concert talks, which not everyone attends. Immediately before the work in question is the most appropriate time for the conductor to speak directly to the audience and address this topic, and to explain their thinking.

What is not going to work is what I hear suggested a lot, that we need to "educate" the audience. Does that sound like a fun night out to you, some guy in a suit comes out and lectures you about what not to do before the concert even begins? It is not realistic for American orchestras in the 21st century. Such attitudes are off-putting and confirm stereotypes people have about orchestras being for snooty rich folks. It is not entirely wrong, but it cannot be done separately from the performance. It must be done as **part** of the performance, by the conductor, and some conductors will be better at it than others. Some musicians would also be effective communicators for this message.

For audience members, my advice is the same as I have read in a quote from conductor Marin Alsop, "Never applaud just because something is over, or in a perfunctory way." Even when applause is appropriate – say, the end of Mahler's Ninth Symphony – that is also a situation where it is not desirable to have it start too soon. Some works inspire immediate responses – other times, even at the end of the work, it is best to let the music sink in and have its space for a moment. But as with dress, please refrain from shaming others. Those treated in such a way are unlikely to return.

Without question, this topic can be daunting to newcomers. It is high time for conductors to deal with this sensitively, but directly.

Cell Phones And Devices

I believe that over time, we will see more uses of devices at concerts. They may be used to follow scores or read program notes during the performances, and the use of a dark screen mode can eliminate the distracting bright light we usually associate with cell phones in the theatre. While more mature folks like me appreciate "a break from screen time," it is unrealistic to expect that rising generations will feel the same way. They want events to be interactive and sharable, and that means a smartphone.

What we cannot have is people talking on their phones during concerts or letting them ring. This is especially bothersome, for it is not that hard to silence a cell phone! No matter, anyone who attends concerts with any regularity has surely experienced the following scenario.
First or second ring: not sure it's their phone. Third or fourth ring: they realize it is theirs and start fumbling for it. Next ring: a loud one when they finally take it out. Finally, it stops.

It is distracting and annoying to literally everyone in the audience. I have even seen someone take a call while seated in the row directly in front of the conductor! "Hello? Yeah, I'm at the symphony."

Even these egregious situations should be handled by house management. I have seen too many halls where the ushers (who may not answer to the orchestra) have no orientation in the environment we try to create around symphonic performances. House management must do a better job, and audience members should refrain from shaming one another; I admit, in these situations, it is not easy.

Children At Concerts

Almost all orchestras offer family programs designed for younger minds and shorter attention spans, often called "Family," "Discovery," "Storytime," or the like. If you are a parent or grandparent wanting to introduce children to orchestral music, these programs are the place to start.
Many other types of programs are not as good a fit for kids. For instance, it is not a good idea to bring your six-year-old to a Bruckner symphony lasting over an hour. I have seen it happen, and while usually well-meaning, it is simply not considerate of others, as well as unfair to the child.

Silence is an important part of the classical music experience, and nothing breaks silence better than a fussy toddler or bored eight-year-old. Only children who are mature enough to sit quietly - for some period, without screens or toys as distractions, without disturbing their neighbors - should be brought to full-length symphonic concerts. As I noted, there will almost certainly be other options from your local orchestra designed with children in mind. Check those out first, before bringing little Johnny to *Das Lied von der Erde*.

Our Biggest Problem

It is not the music! In my opinion, it is all the other baggage that surrounds concertgoing, especially feeling uncomfortable or out of place. Orchestra managements, conductors, and musicians can only do so much. All of us, as audience members, have a responsibility to help others enjoy the live concert experience.

This starts with not looking down on people because of how they are dressed, or because they clapped at the wrong time. It is just not helpful.

When behavior really is disruptive – and sometimes it is longtime concertgoers who are guilty, with such things as talking during the performance – call it to the attention of an usher or the house manager. They are trained to handle such situations.

Be kind and tolerant to your fellow audience members, as there is far too little grace and patience in the world, and we could all do more.

7. TIS THE SEASON

I am an unabashed lover of Christmas, especially Christmas music. I lock in the Christmas stations on Sirius XM as soon as they become available, and I have an extensive collection of Christmas recordings with artists ranging from the Baltimore Consort to Twisted Sister. Similarly, while I read *A Christmas Carol* every year, I have also been known to watch the occasional Hallmark movie. I am also one of those people who never tire of hearing "All I Want for Christmas Is You." Classic or pop, I really can't get enough Christmas.

Some readers may now be questioning my sanity, but I will say this: it is a personality trait that served me well as an orchestra executive, because one thing you can count on orchestras to do is lots and lots of concerts that tie to the winter holiday season.

These events evince a certain amount of eye-rolling or wincing from some in the business, both on and off the stage, but I have looked forward to them. In addition to loving the music, I enjoy them because, in the holiday season, there is no doubt that what we do has an enthusiastic audience, one that will prioritize attendance and participation year in and year out. Holidays are about traditions, and the winter holidays are a time when the sound of an orchestra really connects with popular culture.

It is not only a matter of strong box office, although since management's success is largely measured by numbers, that never hurts; for me, it was firstly the feeling of, "Tonight, we made a lot of people happy." There is simply nothing better than being in the lobby as a happy audience departs, and to be thanked for the concert. That makes a lot of time spent in committee meetings considerably more tolerable!

Familiar traditions. We put up a tree or menorah, we look forward to sharing presents, we plan festive gatherings with friends and relatives. Our traditions may be cultural or religious, or they may be 100% secular, like watching *National Lampoon's Christmas Vacation* or *Die Hard*.

Going to concerts and performances, from kindergarten level to professional orchestra, is also, thankfully, part of the holiday tradition for many. To meet these expectations, our business brings out some tried and true classics: *Messiah*, *The Nutcracker*, *Amahl and the Night Visitors*, any number of works of the great Leroy Anderson.

While I understand that familiarity may occasionally breed some mild disdain ("We're playing 'Sleigh Ride' AGAIN?"), it is precisely that comforting prior acquaintance that draws the crowds back, year after year. Christmas has musical traditions going back over a millennium, and they are far better represented by an orchestra, especially when joined by solo vocalists and a choir, than almost any other ensemble or group that could be imagined.

It is a truth of marketing that people gravitate to, and are more comfortable spending discretionary income upon, things that "they've heard of." A lot of people have heard of *The Nutcracker* and have some idea what a holiday pops concert will be like, and like it or not, for a big slice of the public, the sound of an orchestra equates with the sound of Christmas.

The bottom-line impact is no humbug. When I was with the Dayton Performing Arts Alliance, sales for the Dayton Ballet/ Dayton Philharmonic's annual staging of *The Nutcracker* were typically 25% of the Alliance's overall annual single ticket income and the vast majority of the Ballet's single-ticket income. We spoke of it as our "Super Bowl." Indeed, *The Nutcracker* is the financial backbone for most ballet companies, the one indispensable thing that makes everything else possible.

For orchestras, holiday pops offers similarly great opportunities for strong sales and big audiences. There are numerous approaches – the "hometown holiday" with many performers from the community joining the orchestra or a more standard pops approach with a "name" guest performer are the most common. The potential for boffo box office is so great that orchestras keep finding new ways to keep the holiday juggernaut going. In Dayton, we rolled out "A John Denver Christmas" and "A Charlie Brown Christmas" in addition to our traditional holiday pops. I have been an attendee of the North Carolina Symphony, and I note that they not only do holiday pops, touring holiday pops, Messiah, and Nutcracker, but a recent holiday lineup also included "A Harry Potter Holiday" and "Candlelight Christmas."

Messiah is another perennial favorite – oddly, at least given the story, more so at Christmas than at Easter. December *Messiahs* are often shortened a bit from Handel's original, usually including the Prophecy and Nativity portions, a few favorite arias and choruses from later in the work and ending with the Hallelujah Chorus. That is not what Handel wrote, but as a longtime orchestra manager, I understand about time constraints, overtime, and not going on too long.

I do miss my threefold "Amen" and love it when it is not omitted, but these are mild concerns - anytime there is so much enthusiasm for a 284-year-old true masterpiece, it is a good thing, whatever the cuts and order shuffle may be.

A few of my other personal *Messiah* preferences: I do not think it necessary to take all the repeats in every aria, although I know others prefer that (and that is what Handel wrote, so I admit my inconsistency!). I also appreciate it when conductors keep it moving, without applause after every number – that may shave ten to fifteen minutes off the total run time, depending on how much of the original work you are doing.

Nutcracker is another one that gets all mixed around, based on different choreographers' takes on the story. There are probably more different sequences for the first act party scene than lights on the tree. I can think of few things more likely to make an orchestra librarian's heart beat faster than the prospect of a new set of cuts for *The Nutcracker*.

I mentioned that *The Nutcracker i*s the bread-and-butter essential work for every ballet company in the country, and they all depend on the revenue it generates to fund all their other activities. With that said, while I have no issue with shorter repertoire works, especially new ones, being done to a recording, a masterpiece orchestral score like Tchaikovsky's deserves to have a full orchestra to play it. I sympathize with the additional financial challenge this brings to companies not accustomed to doing the work in this manner. One of the things I am most proud of that we accomplished with the Dayton Performing Arts Alliance was putting the Dayton Philharmonic back in the pit for Dayton Ballet's Nutcracker. It was a real "aha" moment in terms of the community understanding the value of this new alliance and partnership, and the ticket sales rose dramatically from the prior season.

On that cheerful note, when December rolls around again, I hope all in the orchestra business enjoy the holiday season and see it for what it is – a great annual opportunity to remind everyone of the unique power and beauty of orchestral music, and of the special joy that musicians and great music bring to our lives.

8. THE MODERN MAESTRO: CHANGING ATTITUDES AROUND THE CONDUCTOR'S ROLE

Conductors have been much in the news in recent years. At a time when classical music does not get much attention in popular culture, we saw two much-discussed movies center around conductors, both fictional and real-life. First was the critically acclaimed 2022 film *Tár,* in which Cate Blanchett gave a memorable performance as the titular maestro. In 2024, we saw *Maestro,* starring Bradley Cooper as Leonard Bernstein, a convincing and critically acclaimed performance.

Real-life conductors made headlines for less comfortable reasons. There were several prominent "#MeToo" cases involving conductors, and a major music conservatory faced an outright student revolt over alleged behavior of their principal conductor. The conductor in question was accused of sexual harassment, cleared by a Title IX investigation, but still seen as so strongly objectionable by students that they refused to rehearse or perform with him, citing a hostile atmosphere and bullying.

Conductors are challenging for orchestras. The role is exceptionally difficult from an artistic standpoint, and we also count on the conductor, particularly with smaller orchestras, to be the orchestra's avatar in the community and all-around ambassador, promoter, cheerleader, and fundraiser.

It is hard to do all these responsibilities well. Some conductors connect well with their musicians but are unable to work effectively with their board or to charm donors. Others are so effective at charming donors that poor relationships with their orchestras are tolerated for a long time. Some do succeed in putting the whole package together. Orchestras with such a conductor should cherish every minute of the experience.

Orchestras often tie their identity strongly to that of their music director. A lot of season brochures put the conductor right on the front cover, and the conductor's face is often prominently featured in advertising of all kinds. There are good reasons for this – the conductor is the most visible person on stage, and it is easier to build identity around that one front-and-center person than around a group picture of seventy-five people. The conductor is (correctly) viewed as a leader in the cultural community and one that other leaders and influential people want to know.

Orchestras have generally benefited from this. I have often said that the two things that are real game changers for orchestras are new halls and new conductors. The right conductor at the right time can bring a groundswell of public interest and enthusiasm. Suddenly an orchestra's concerts can become "the place to be," and people are talking about the orchestra with excitement again. This is precisely what those who lead orchestras want to see.

We thus place huge responsibility in the hands of the conductor and frequently allow her or him to carry a good deal of the orchestra's public image. It takes a certain amount of ego to do this, most of all to get up in front of a full concert hall and lead an orchestra of highly trained, highly gifted musicians as the primary interpreter of the music. We need that ego on the stage, so we make allowances for what is generally called "the artistic temperament" when off the stage. A lot of that is tolerance for benign things, like not being surprised if the conductor isn't always on time for meetings or changes his/her mind a lot regarding programming.

There has been a dark side to this as well. Conductors used to have tremendous, unchecked power. There is an old joke in the field that asking a musician which conductor they favor is like asking a mouse which cat they like best. In the old days, tyrannical conductors like Toscanini could indeed dismiss a musician for one wrong note. Union protections put an end to that sort of extreme power, but many conductors were happy to still be regarded with fear by their musicians.

They could still get away with a lot. I think there are few roles where we have historically been more likely to excuse bad behavior than orchestral conductor, particularly when the role is held by a white man. Up until very recently, there has remained a broad tolerance for temper tantrums, visible displays of anger and frustration, and personal singling-out.

Why has this been? We buy into the "maestro" image of the conductor as the guardian of tradition and high standards, and thus fully entitled to vent displeasure in any way they see fit. There's been a tendency to view the conductor as a sort of tough coach or drill sergeant, someone who must bring order out of chaos and is allowed to express himself as necessary to accomplish this goal. We view the conductor as someone with almost mystical abilities and thus to be regarded with a sort of awe not generally accorded to mere mortals.

Going back to popular culture, this trope has certainly had some resonance, whether it is the whispered anticipation of "Leopold!" in Fantasia or Steinfeld's mercurial "Maestro." My personal favorite comedic caricature of this otherworldly, unpredictable persona is the fictional conductor Max Beissart as portrayed by former ballet dancer Alexander Godunov (also seen in *Die Hard*) in the 1986 film *The Money Pit*. If you have not seen it, it's worth seeing for this very funny performance alone; it also features the young Tom Hanks. However, as many musicians can tell you, there is nothing funny about being on stage with a conductor who's having a tantrum.

The workplace of the 2020s is very different from the workplace of 1973. Over the course of thirty years as an Executive Director, I had to learn my own lessons about the role of anger in leadership, and my conclusion is there is basically no place for it. Passion, yes – anger, no. One must lead in a positive, encouraging, empathetic way. While some conductors have been slow to realize it, this is true in the orchestral workplace as well.

Like most behavioral issues, it is generational. If a conductor, as a younger musician or conducting student, saw sarcasm, ridicule, and anger as part of how they were taught, even if it made them uncomfortable, my observation is that conductor is more likely to turn to that sort of behavior in challenging moments. Fortunately, as societal standards have changed, fewer and fewer conductors are around who still approach their work in that way. Fewer now were trained that way, so they do not do it when they themselves are in positions of responsibility. A greater presence for women and people of color on the podium is also changing the paradigm and further diminishing the profession's more toxic traditions.

Circling back to *Tár*, the film attracted a good deal of criticism, justifiably so, for showing a female conductor as toxic and predatory when historically the profession, including offenders in those areas, has been almost exclusively male. That is still the case more so than in most professions, but I'm encouraged to note that the most exciting, compelling new conductors I have recently encountered have all been women.

The conductor who can successfully lead in our times is the best prepared musician on stage, with a comprehensive knowledge of the score, yet that knowledge is never presented in an arrogant or patronizing way. They are aware of the challenges that confront each section and sensitive to them – for instance, understanding that particularly difficult brass passages or pages and pages of string tremolo may not be played full out in a rehearsal on the same day as a concert. They focus more on what they hear that they like and how to get more of that, rather than focusing with negativity on what they don't like and how to discourage it. They inspire an orchestra to be more than the sum of its parts, to trust in its collective ability, and to approach performances with excitement and joy.

I fully believe that this style can bring just as strong a result as the old-school, fear-based "reign of terror" approach. In time, it will become the new normal, and that will be a positive development for our field. The conductor of today brings new perspectives, insight, and lived experiences, and that is without question a good thing.

9. THE EVOLVING ROLE OF THE EXECUTIVE DIRECTOR

In my first chapter about the four constituencies of the orchestra organization, I touched briefly on the role of the Executive Director. I described that person as the "overall administrative director and all-around leader for the organization."

What that means in practice varies widely, depending on the size of the organization. With smaller orchestras, the Executive Director (ED) may be a jack-of-all-trades who does everything from ordering the music to mailing out the tickets. With the very largest orchestras, the ED may be more like a college president, with their attention focused on the largest donors and the most strategic priorities and little to no day-to-day operating responsibility.

The ED's role will evolve as the organization grows, has changing needs, and adjusts its staffing accordingly.

I experienced this in my own career. My first positions as an Executive Director were with orchestras in the $1 million annual budget range. With groups of that size, my duties were inwardly focused: coordination of schedules, hiring and logistics for guest artists, labor relations, budgeting, grant writing and reporting, and management of the other staff members. They included many things that would be managed at the departmental level in a bigger organization, like grant writing, typically part of the development office, and guest artist support, typically the responsibility of an operations office. However, if your operations staff is just a part-time music librarian and a part-time orchestra personnel manager, you will be doing much of this work yourself.

And so, I did. I made hotel and air reservations for the orchestra's soloists. I met them at the airport and drove them to their hotel, and back and forth to rehearsals. I picked them up on the night of the concert and got them backstage. My most memorable experience was serving as chauffeur for legendary soprano Kathleen Battle. At the time she appeared with my orchestra, she had a reputation for being, shall we say, somewhat touchy. However, I found her to be very lovely and enjoyed my time with her. But was I nervous at the outset? I certainly was!

I also remember very clearly the challenge of writing a National Endowment for the Arts grant application, completely on my own, in my first year as a new Executive Director. It is a lot of information to pull together, and every box must be checked.

As time went on, I needed to spend more time with other priorities: planning with the music director, fundraising with the board, and representing the orchestra in the community. Since my orchestra was growing, I was able to hire more staff—first an Executive Assistant who could take care of the guest artists, then eventually a grant writer to tackle all the various applications. Most orchestras will have a state arts agency application every year, plus the NEA, if they choose to apply, and several local applications; these could be city or county applications, or to a United Arts Fund. These can be managed exclusively by the Executive Director only in small situations where the other demands are not too great. Having additional help meant I was able to spend my time on the things where my personal involvement could make the most difference.

Whatever the situation, every orchestra ED needs a mix of outward- and inward-facing skills. The exact balance will be determined by the organization's size and longevity as, oftentimes, new organizations begin without any staff at all, with everything done by volunteers. As time goes by, there is a need for a dedicated professional and that is when the first ED gets hired. They start handling all day-to-day responsibilities but eventually, if the orchestra is able to grow, they will add additional staff as direct reports, to ensure that the work gets done without it being an unsustainable load on any one person.

This means, though, that the same personality that is a good fit for that jack-of-all-trades, do-it- all-yourself role typical for new organization directors may not be a great fit for a later-stage organization where a more strategic, outward-facing leader is needed.

All EDs have strengths and weaknesses; if you are in a situation where you have staff reporting to you, the key is to surround yourself with people who will complement your strengths and help compensate for any weaknesses. For instance, a very outward-focused, meeting-and-greeting style ED will want a strong general manager or COO to keep track of the details, and a more inward-focused strategist will want the partnership of a strong Development Director to make sure they are connected to the right people.

A challenge is that different constituencies may have different ideas of what is most needed from the Executive Director at any given time. Boards want to see financial stability including ticket sales and fundraising success. Conductors want attention to special artistic initiatives and support for adventurous programming. Volunteers want attention, recognition, and visible support for their events. Staff want a mentor and a leader who will have their back. Musicians want all of the above, and ongoing improvements in their contracts, as well.

Further, the needs may be perceived differently by the Board when new Board leadership is elected, and since the ED reports to the

Board, the ED may suddenly confront a need to change style or find a new situation.

Another challenging aspect can be that, whether they will say it aloud or not, there is an expectation from some constituents that you "look the part," and unfortunately, for many, that still means a white guy with the "executive look," i.e. tall, trim, well-groomed, wearing only white or pale blue shirts with plain pattern ties and dark suits. This can be an unstated expectation for board leaders, as well, with many biased toward a straight-from-central-casting "CEO" type. The field does have a track record with strong female leaders, and I am hopeful that these executive stereotypes from the mid-twentieth century may eventually be cast aside.

When I left my last position, I tried to summarize what I thought was most needed for that orchestra at that time in its history and budgetary growth (in this case, an annual budget of about $6 million). I came up with several "have 'x,' but not at the expense of 'y' statements," as follows:

The ED should have an outgoing personality and be a good fundraiser and external representative, but not at the expense of managerial skills in the office.

The ED should be a detail-oriented internal manager, but not at the expense of representing the orchestra well externally.

The ED must have strong artistic knowledge including repertoire, programming, instrumentation, conductors, and soloists, not at the expense of business skills.

The ED must have a solid background in business including marketing, fundraising, accounting, cash management, employment practices, HR, and employee benefits, but not at the expense of passion for the artistic mission.

The ED must have a clear-eyed focus on the bottom line, but not at the expense of staff and musicians. Similarly, the ED must have a sympathetic and supportive relationship with musicians and staff, but not at the expense of the fiscal interests of the organization.

The ED must be able to lead and mentor staff, but not at the expense of external relationships with board members and donors. The ED must be able to relate comfortably to wealthy, older donors but still seem approachable to younger, entry level staff. The ED must have equally strong "people skills" with Silent Generation through Gen Z.

The ED must be a strong believer in and promoter of arts education programs. Musical training is highly desirable, and a financial background, especially familiarity with non-profit accounting, is essential.

So, it is a balancing act, with many aspects of the job that can at times be in conflict, one with the other. Further, while you strive to achieve what you feel is the right blend, it may not be the blend that others perceive as necessary.

This is usually the point where I say, "Arts management is not for the faint of heart." I do want to emphasize one other point from the above. Few things have served me as well in my arts management career as my study of graduate level accounting and finance. It was a cold shower shock to take those courses after majoring in music, but I am glad I did. It is so important for the ED to thoroughly understand the numbers and be able to interpret and explain them to others. You cannot rely on others to know in which direction the ship is headed; you must be able to see it for yourself.

It is not an easy role at the personal level. You are typically not really a peer with your board members, who have hired you, but you are not a peer with staff and musicians, either, who always know where the buck stops. You are caught in a sort of middle zone where you are an employee to some and the "evil overlord" to others. So always remember, there are others around the country who are doing the same thing and facing the same challenges, and others in your community who are doing the job with similar organizations. I advise all new Executive Directors to network well; the perspective of others can be immensely helpful in difficult situations.

What is the one skill I wish I had come into the profession with? I know I would have been well-served to have taken up golf, and I am not kidding. That, and to be taller, and I am kidding/not kidding about that one.

I experienced and did a lot in thirty years as an Executive Director and have many pleasant memories as well as experiences I would care not to repeat. For anyone seeking guidance, my professional contact information appears elsewhere in this volume.

10. WORKERS OF THE WORLD TUNE-UP: LABOR RELATIONS

Over the past forty years, union membership in the United States has fallen dramatically. In 1983, twenty percent of the American workforce belonged to a union; in 2023, it was down to ten percent.

It is worth noting that the overall ten percent level is driven by a much higher percentage – thirty-eight percent – of union membership by the workforce in the public sector: people like teachers, firefighters, and police officers. In the private sector, only seven percent of workers belong to a union.

This is interesting to me, because when I think of a union worker, I think first of an auto or steel worker, definitely private sector companies. I am of the generation old enough to remember when those industries were still strong in this country, with robust union membership earning good middle-class wages. Now, those industries have been decimated by overseas competition.

It might surprise some people to learn that one field where union membership is almost universal in the US is symphony orchestras, more specifically professional symphony orchestra musicians. If musicians are being compensated for their services at any level of significance, the chances are they are doing so under a union contract with the American Federation of Musicians (AFM), the national union that represents musicians. These contracts, negotiated by the union on behalf of its members, are referred to as "Collective Bargaining Agreements" or "CBAs."

Like most unions, the AFM has a national organization as well as various "locals" in different communities. In a typical AFM local, the majority of the dues and overall membership comes from the musicians of that community's professional orchestra. In terms of numbers, orchestras are "where the action is" for the musicians' union. There are studio musicians in cities with recording industry activity and session musicians in LA in the film and television industry, but in most AFM locals, orchestra musicians have great influence as the primary generators of dues. (Orchestra musicians typically pay annual membership dues as well as "work dues," which are a percentage of earnings sent to the union each time work is compensated under a union contract).

This is a very important topic for newcomers to the field. If you are a musician, you will be joining the union, and even if you are in a right-to-work state, where union membership may not be required, you will still most likely be working under the terms of a union contract.

If you are an executive director or staff member, you will be dealing with the union and union rules in some way, perhaps in a major way depending on your specific job responsibilities. You should also be aware of a possible dynamic involving board attitudes towards organized labor. Many of your board members will be from the executive or business-owning class. This is appropriate; these are civic leaders who are there to support one of their community's cultural treasures, and they have the power of the purse to provide meaningful funding support. However, in some cases, they also come in with a negative opinion of unions, and sometimes, even as you bargain for management, you will need to educate board members about the union and the realities of collective bargaining work agreements.

Finally, if you are a board member, you are now part of the

governance of a business with a collective bargaining agreement, meaning your business is subject to rules of the National Labor Relations Board. It is a serious matter, and it has distressed me to see some board members who come into an organization not fully aware of the orchestra's union status, or even that the musicians are paid.

Each orchestra's CBA is worked out through formal contract negotiations every few years. CBAs usually cover 3-5 years, although shorter terms may be agreed upon in times of unusual change, challenge, or uncertainty. During negotiations, the musicians are represented by their elected representatives from within their ranks, usually referred to as the "Orchestra" or "Players" Committee, as well as representatives of the local union, and, if the orchestra is of at least "regional orchestra" size, a negotiator from the national AFM organization.

Orchestra management is typically represented in negotiations by the Executive Director and some members of the operations or finance staff, ideally along with some board members. I think it is extremely healthy for the board to have a presence at negotiations. They should defer to management when the issues are very orchestra-specific, but I have benefited time and time again from the broader perspective and life experience of a board member working with me at the bargaining table. It is also helpful when presenting the status or results of negotiations to the board, if one of their members has been part of the process.

In addition, some managements may also specifically engage a labor lawyer as part of their negotiating team, or one of the board members who participates may have this expertise.

I worked with the union as an orchestra executive director for thirty years and have lost count of the number of collective bargaining agreements I negotiated. As you might expect, I have a variety of feelings about the union. As an individual, I believe unions have been good for workers in this country. As others have said, if you like having weekends or days off in general, thank a union; if you're fortunate enough to have employer-provided health insurance, thank a union; if you get paid vacation or sick days, thank a union. None of those things were widespread until workers bargained for them, using their collective power as a group, with their employers.

For musicians, unions offered more than just an opportunity to collectively bargain for wages. They allowed musicians to bargain for work conditions that would be safe, both for themselves and their instruments; they provided some element of job security or at least due process, should a conductor become upset with them. Few of us would like to be in a job where the literal equivalent of one wrong note could cost us our livelihood; that was the reality for orchestra musicians before they unionized.

Turning back to the labor movement as a whole, it was often a literal fight for workers to gain those benefits, which employers were often reluctant to grant. I lived in West Virginia for twelve years and gained a real appreciation there for the value of unions and the struggle of workers for fair pay and decent working conditions. Working in a coal mine is hard, dangerous, uncomfortable work. Imagine doing it in a company town where you were paid in company scrip rather than real money; it is only about a hundred years ago when that was a reality. Most astonishingly, the only time US Air Force bomber aircraft have been used on domestic targets was during a bloody labor dispute (Battle of Blair Mountain, 1921; another part of American history that was never taught).

So while I personally support most of the aims of the labor movement, as an orchestra executive, I've had my share of "shaking my head" moments with the union (fortunately none of them involving battles or bombers). You might think "compensation" would be the biggest headache. Although it may take the most time at the negotiating table, once it is agreed upon, it becomes routine. You set up the payroll system with the right numbers and it becomes automatic; your biggest headache then becomes raising the money to pay for it, but that is a different topic!

The troublesome issues usually have to do with work rules and the interpretation of the same. You will encounter a lot of situations of "this wording means this" countered by "no, it was intended to mean this" and work on finding compromise; if you cannot find informal compromise, CBAs always provide for a formal grievance and arbitration procedure for the most challenging disputes. Flash points are often around the topics of overtime, absence, and showing up late; work conditions such as temperature and stage setup; hiring order and when certain players must be called versus another player "doubling"; and scheduling and the timing of changes to the schedule.

That last one can really bite you; most CBAs do not allow for changes, at least without penalty, within a certain period of time, like thirty days, prior to a given event. There are few things worse for a manager than discovering a typo in the schedule when it is now too late, under the CBA, to make a change. For this reason, it is important for persons working in operations, including personnel managers, librarians, and operations managers, to be highly detail-oriented and literal. I can sometimes be irritating to my significant other by being very specific about time ("We didn't leave at 7:30; it was 7:36"), but that is precisely the kind of accuracy focus that served me well in my orchestra career. Just as in the rental car commercial, CBA work rules are an area where "close enough" will not do.

I think it is very important to be clear-eyed about the labor-management relationship in orchestras. My approach is to understand it as a benignly adversarial relationship, united in the end by common interests. There has been a lot to talk in recent years about mutual interest bargaining and other supposed alternatives to traditional, position-based bargaining. In my view, position-based bargaining, in a climate of mutual respect, is the best way to discover mutual interests. Anytime someone wants to start by declaring mutual interests, I suspect they have already decided what those interests are and are seeking to use the process to guide matters to their own advantage.

Of course, that is a fair description of how one often exerts influence as an executive, and in candor, if I had my druthers, I would have sought to be a benign, magnanimous dictator throughout my orchestra career. That is why we have cautionary tales about how power corrupts, whether tragic like the fall of Anakin Skywalker in *Star Wars* or banal like the antics of Michael Scott in *The Office*. I would further say that as tempting as that approach might seem, my experience is that organizations are stronger when employees have a genuine voice and some degree of power in the organization. Those things are sometimes necessary to guarantee that their employer will truly listen and take their opinions and preferences into account. There are times when the interests of the employees do not fully align with those of the organization as a whole, but the healthiest organizations never lose sight of their employees' interests.

The labor-management dynamic in orchestras, at its best, can bring about that balance. At its worse, of course, it becomes rival camps, each suspicious and mistrustful of the motives of the other.

The best way to counteract that, or to keep it from coming to pass in the first place, is full candor and honesty about the realities of the organization. Share the numbers. Share the challenges. Be honest about audience preferences and funder mandates. Further, there is never, ever, a way to make it work without genuine respect on both sides. As an orchestra executive, you must earn your respect; but if you come into the job without preexisting respect for musical artists, you are in the wrong job.

While you will hear your share of horror stories about bad behavior in negotiations, on the part of both labor and management, my experience has always been that candor and respect will lead to a successful outcome.

While I have lost count of my negotiating experiences, which included the stagehands' union or IATSE as well as the AFM, my first memory of all of them is of that moment when you smile and shake hands and realize that you have found a compromise that everyone can live with. Through a detailed process of sharing concerns, challenges, and sometimes vigorous debate, you have emerged with an agreement to move forward.

That is the American way, when we find common interests and work together even though we may not agree on everything. I am proud to have been a part of it.

11. YOU OUGHT TO KNOW

As I have noted in previous chapters, there is immense potential for misunderstanding between the constituents of symphony orchestras, because of their tendency to function in silos, each doing their own thing, without necessarily a clear view of what the other parts are doing.

As I worked with orchestras, I became aware of several things, as a staff member, that board members and musicians wanted me to know. In turn, I saw several areas where those same groups needed to see it from the perspective of the staff.

In this chapter, I will summarize those impressions of the things each constituency often feels is not understood by the other – what they would "like you to know."

Board Members

Many board members have a genuine love of music and artistic expression. They are there to support that endeavor.

Board members are uncompensated volunteers; in addition, they are expected to be among the orchestra's most generous donors. They are putting their money where their mouth is and should be treated with the appropriate respect for that commitment. It is not something to be taken for granted, or for advantage; while board members and other major donors are often genuine music lovers, I have never met one who saw herself as a human ATM.

Board members are typically busy people. They are leaders in their professions, in demand for other boards and volunteer positions, and they may have a family. Their time has value. It is incumbent on the orchestras they serve not to waste it.

All constituents must understand that orchestras are non-profits; they are not paying dividends to shareholders. The community are the shareholders, and the board is there to represent the community. The "dividends" are the cultural and educational service the orchestra provides to the community. With no cash dividends being paid, no one is making a "profit." The salaries paid, even to top staff, are not profits, they are expenses. Profits would be any amount remaining after all expenses have been paid, and orchestras still have lots of expenses remaining after all the revenue is in. That is why they are non-profits and depend on the generosity of various donors and funders to stay afloat. Everyone involved needs to understand that sixty cents of every dollar an orchestra spends came from a voluntary contribution. It is a fragile business model, and one where the old parable about the goose that laid the golden eggs applies.

Board members, whether called "Directors" or "Trustees," are in fact entrusted by the community with the long-term preservation of the organization. As such, when they exhibit concern over fiscal matters, it is not because they are cheap, or stingy, or mean; it is because they want to be sure the organization does not make choices that may impair its future viability. The best Board members understand their own obligation to help find and generate the revenue that is just as important as expense management to that future success.

Musicians

Musicians face enormous pressure to always be at their best, every rehearsal, every performance. There is far less tolerance for an "off day" than in most other professions. It's more analogous to being a surgeon; you've got to do it right, or there will be consequences. While a musician cannot kill someone by missing a note, they can certainly lose an audition, or embarrass the orchestra with a subpar performance.

The hours spent rehearsing and performing are just the beginning, in terms of the time they invest in their position in the orchestra. In addition, many hours of individual practice and preparation are required. This varies from concert to concert, depending on the repertoire and whether the musician has played it before, but is always necessary. Oboes and bassoonists also spend many hours making their own reeds. It is thus offensive to musicians to imply that they "only work twenty hours a week" or similar statement.

The equipment required to perform in a symphony orchestra can be quite costly. Most people have heard of golden era string instruments, exemplified by the work of Stradivari, being worth millions, but many might be surprised to learn that the bows required to play those instruments can also cost into six figures. While woodwind and brass instruments are typically far less costly, the finest may still cost as much as some people would expect to spend on a car. Further, double-reed players must invest in equipment and raw materials to make their own reeds; single-reed players can just buy them, but that usually means purchasing boxes and boxes of reeds and finding one or two they like in an entire box. Brass and percussion players usually own multiple instruments, and large instruments like harp and double bass require large vehicles to transport them. The only members of the orchestra who don't typically provide their own instruments are pianists and percussionists; but of course, they need to have one at home on which to practice, so that even though the orchestra may own the piano or timpani they use in performances, they are nonetheless investing in their own instruments.

Musicians in smaller, per-service orchestras usually play in more than one, as the compensation from just one per-service orchestra is typically less than a living wage. To do this, many are "road warriors," putting thousands and thousands of miles on their vehicles every year, going back and forth from commitments in multiple states.

I mentioned musicians being comparable to surgeons. Other analogous professions – because they require years of training and a great deal of innate natural talent – include professional athletes and top courtroom litigators. Compensation for musicians, however, is usually far less than in those comparable fields. The best-paid musicians in the largest orchestras are paid salaries that would seem middling to low for the type of specialized professions I have mentioned above. Further, for per-service musicians – because every position they hold, even if they hold several simultaneously, may be construed as "part-time" – there may be no benefits at all. Imagine trying to raise a family without employer-provided health insurance. Imagine being an older musician and facing a heart attack or a cancer diagnosis without insurance, or with just the minimum required by law. We hear a lot about the "gig economy" these days; many orchestral musicians have been living that reality for years.

Why do they do it? For many, it is a calling, much as it is for deeply committed staff. Musicians are aware they could apply their intelligence and work ethic to be more successful or financially rewarded in a "normal" job, but they still prefer to just keep making ends meet, for the love of making music. Others should view it as a feature, not a bug, by which I mean something that should be appreciated and rewarded to the maximum extent possible, not something by which musicians may be taken advantage of.

Direct Service Volunteers

As I noted, many orchestra volunteer associations began as "women's associations" at a time when women typically did not participate in governance activities reserved for men. As such, they did a great deal of the work of symphony orchestras, especially as these associations mostly got their start at a time before orchestras became more professionalized, particularly in the area of fundraising.

Volunteer associations were often largely responsible for the season ticket campaign; now, in many places, they may participate in some renewal reminder phone-a-thons, but the rest is now handled by professional box office and marketing teams.

Similarly, while annual galas, golf tournaments, and designer showhouses used to raise significant contributed income for orchestras, these have now been proportionally diminished by ever-expanding fundraising directed at both individual and corporate sources.

One area where volunteer associations continue to play a strong role is in education programs. Volunteers make significant contributions to orchestra educational efforts as classroom presenters or docents, and with the very labor-intensive process of shepherding thousands of schoolchildren in and out of the concert hall for education concerts.

Most orchestra volunteers are older and recall the times when their efforts were seen as more important. As a result, they often feel unappreciated and taken for granted. This is a very sensitive area, especially for younger people coming into the field who have never worked with a regular volunteer before. "Who exactly are these people, do I report to them, and if not, why do I have to put up with them?" is the candid way I would characterize the feedback I often received, as an ED, from newer members of my staff regarding volunteers.

What I think orchestra volunteers want, especially in a time of changing roles and purpose for their organizations, is appreciation. They deserve it; these are giving freely of their time out of love for the organization and its mission. Many of the projects that orchestra volunteers mount year in and year out are very labor intensive, akin to full-time jobs for those that chair these projects. I have nothing but respect for such people, and I fear that, as the years go by, we will not see their like again.

Staff

The hours are long, and while salaries are paid, which may look like a good deal (especially to per-service musicians), those salaries are usually at the bottom of the wage scale, even for entry-level jobs. Many arts organizations offer hourly wages for entry-level positions that are comparable to those in the fast-food industry.

In addition, benefits, particularly at regional per-service orchestras, are not competitive with the private sector. This includes both health, dental, and vision insurance, and especially retirement. I worked for five different orchestras for over thirty-three years. In that entire time, I never received a single pension or retirement contribution from my employer, not even a match, not even a match up to a certain percentage – my only option for a pension contribution was whatever amount I chose, voluntarily, to take out of my own pay. Keep in mind that at four of those orchestras, I was the Executive Director, the position one would expect to have the most "perks." (I never got my own parking space, either, but I can joke about that one).

Unlike many jobs in the private sector, weekends for staff are usually not a real thing; because that is when the performances take place, and when orchestra staff are most needed. Take off Monday, you say? That is when the phone rings the most, from patrons, vendors, and other constituents, so that is not a practical strategy. When I started my first position as an Executive Director, I was advised to work normal hours during the summer as much as possible, "because once that season starts in September, you don't come up for air till May," and that advice was right on the money.

Many orchestra staff members are exceptionally dedicated to the art form. They are aware they could command higher pay and benefits in the private sector, with more reasonable hours, but they choose to stay with orchestras nonetheless, because it is work that is truly meaningful to them. If they do not have that elevated level of dedication, they will almost certainly leave for greener pastures.

This happens a lot with development staff; as an Executive Director, I found it often a struggle to keep good fundraisers from being snapped up by university and hospital foundations, offering better pay and benefits and most weekends "off," rather than "on." For those who view orchestra work as a calling, again, that sentiment is a feature, not a bug, and not a sign that they "couldn't cut it" in the business world, or other similar derisive comment.

Being a not-for-profit is not something to be ashamed of, or a sign of some type of business failure. It is simply a recognition that the service the organization provides is not something that can be supported by market forces alone. There is no "market" that will pay for free concerts for children; it requires subsidy. Further, even though orchestras sell tickets to their various public series, the cost of maintaining a professional symphony orchestra far exceeds what can be generated by ticket sales and other earned income, which comes to about forty percent of the expenses. I encountered board members in my time who did not seem familiar with the non-profit model; or who were under the impression that orchestras were different because of the sale of tickets.

Formal orientations and training for each constituency are important. I write this small book in hope of providing a resource that may prove helpful to newcomers to orchestra organizations. The best education, though, happens when the various constituencies spend time getting to know one another and understanding the sometimes-painful realities of the field. We must avoid the temptation to form the proverbial circular firing squad; heading into an uncertain future, as Benjamin Franklin said, "we must all hang together, or surely we will all hang separately."

12. AL CODA? ORCHESTRAS CONFRONT THE FUTURE

I recently attended the opening night concert of my local symphony orchestra, something I have done every September or October for the past thirty-four years. There is always a sense of renewal and optimism as a new season begins, much like beginning a new school year or athletic season.

Yet there are many challenges facing professional orchestras, in an environment that may prove more hostile than US orchestras have faced before. While I have no doubt that some orchestras will last well into the future, I also feel the field may have reached its high-water mark and may now face a period of gradual decline, in which at least an equal number of orchestras will falter.

It is true that the demise of symphony orchestras has been predicted for quite a while, and one can easily find articles from fifty to sixty years ago fretting about grey heads in the audience and falling interest in the traditional performing arts. Orchestras have proven stubbornly resilient; with a few exceptions, even in the worst cases, where an orchestra has collapsed and gone out of business, there is always a new group starting up within a year or so. The track record, to date, does point to ongoing vitality.

Further, there is no issue with interest in music. Thanks to the internet, great performances are more accessible than ever. In 1974, to find a particular orchestral recording, one would have to browse the bins of a specialized and well-stocked record shop, typically found only in college towns or larger cities. In 2025, with a few clicks of a mouse or taps on a screen, performances of astonishing quality – both audio and video – are readily accessible to all. Talented young people continue to devote themselves to musical studies, and conservatories continue to churn out graduates, in greater numbers than vacant orchestral positions at any given time. Orchestras do not face a supply shortage for performers.

As to the audience, it is true that concerns over aging audiences are a cliché in the orchestra business. So are concerns about competition from in-home entertainment; the current fretting over streaming services has parallels in much older predictions that radio broadcasts and phonograph records would spell doom for live concerts.

Comforting as these reflections may be, they are also a case of saying that because something has worked out before, it will continue to work out in the future, and that is not always how it plays out. Sometimes, certain inflection points arrive, habits change, and industries do change forever. A frequently cited contemporary example is the once-ubiquitous Blockbuster video store, wiped out by streaming, or that well-stocked physical record store, similarly flattened by online alternatives. I also think about passenger rail travel, rendered an anachronism by the rise of airlines and the interstate highway system.

It is my belief that there are certain new developments and phenomena that make the orchestra's place in the twenty-first century more precarious than in the late twentieth, which I further believe will be seen in hindsight as its high-water mark.

In his 2005 book *Collapse: How Societies Choose to Fail or Succeed*, author Jared Diamond examines past civilizations that declined and fell, including the Norse settlers of Greenland, the Anasazi and Mayan Native Americans, and the Easter Islanders of the Pacific. He sees five common factors leading to societal collapse. These are damage to the environment, climate change, hostile neighbors, loss of contact with or loss of support from friendly neighbors, and the choices society makes to respond to those issues. For instance, although surrounded by oceans teeming with fish, the Greenland Norse never really tapped this as a source of food. Instead, they continued trying to farm cattle and raise the same crops that had worked for their ancestors in Scandinavia, leading to disastrous food shortages and hunger. They stuck with what they thought worked, even when it did not work anymore.

I found Diamond's book thought-provoking, and I have begun to think a similar set of factors may be identified that pose a threat to orchestras, as follows: Changing Funder Priorities, Economic Shocks, Culture War Issues, Future Public Health Emergencies, Climate Change, and Internal Strife. I will discuss each one.

Changing Funder Priorities

In the first decade of the twenty-first century, those of us who worked regularly with family foundations and other private funders of the arts noticed a phenomenon of some concern. As one decision-making generation entered its eighties, it began to cede fiscal control to its children: people in their thirties, forties, and fifties. This new generation, even if they acknowledged what their parents had found important, did not necessarily share their parents' values. Rather than providing ongoing support to institutions, like orchestras and museums, they preferred projects, and to vary what they would support from year to year, rather than maintaining consistent support of the same causes. They also began to prioritize social needs and causes over the traditional arts, a case of choosing the urgent over the important. While many funders have more than adequate resources to do

both, their giving will reflect their values, and when the decision-makers no longer see inherent value in the arts, trouble is on the way.
Similarly, institutional funders also began to shift. They embraced year-to-year project funding, rather than ongoing institutional support. There was also often a shift from a general sense of arts and culture being good for communities to priorities based around "outcomes," "impact," and other philanthropic buzz words. There were also buzz words funders wished to avoid, notably "elitism," and it is never hard to, fairly or unfairly, pin that word on the traditional performing arts.

My least favorite of these words is "sustainability." Suddenly, it was not enough to have a worthy project accomplished within a given year. One now had to demonstrate that the project and the organization would still be thriving ten years from now. As others have said, when one chooses to go to a new restaurant, you do so because you have heard the food is good, not because you have heard they have a great five-year plan for growth. Of course, a constant demand for plans, projections, and proposals is good business for arts administrators. What it is not is art, which is where the focus ought to be.

One hundred years ago, there was wealth around transportation, banking, oil, and heavy manufacturing, and titans of industry with names like Carnegie, Fisher, Severance, and Mellon became synonymous with generous philanthropic support of the arts. Today, the money is in tech, and that sector has mostly spent its money in, shall we say, less beneficial ways. It is very different from the philanthropists of the past. It is my belief that orchestras, as a field, will increasingly struggle to make their case to a new generation of funders both public and private.

SUMMARY: A new generation of philanthropists and funding decision-makers may not value the traditional performing arts in the same way as their predecessors, and funding may decline accordingly.

Economic Shocks And Disruptions

Talk about bad timing. After I was named the new President of the Dayton Philharmonic, the first board meeting I attended, in September 2008, was the week of the Bear Stearns collapse. By the time I was fully on the job, a month later, it was clear that a full-scale financial system meltdown was underway.

I had hopes to improve finances with an endowment campaign, having had success with just such a drive with my previous orchestra. We conducted a feasibility study for such a campaign in November to December 2008, and the findings were sobering.

Just as orchestra endowments took a big hit in the stock market implosion underway at the time, so did the net worth of affluent individuals. In discussing their capacity to give as part of our study, many were visibly shaken by the losses they experienced. It quickly became clear that only a much more modest sort of campaign had any chance of success in that environment.

The aftershocks from the 2008 to 2009 market disaster reverberated for the next several years, as various orchestras reported severe financial distress and there were strikes and lockouts as some orchestras tried to scale back. In Dayton, the impact reverberates to this day, as the 2008 to 2009 hard times were a proximate cause of the merger of the Dayton Ballet, Opera, and Philharmonic to form the Dayton Performing Arts Alliance, to date the only three-way arts merger in the United States.

As I will touch on shortly, COVID-19 was a similar shock to orchestras, even though the stock market went up during the pandemic, due to COVID's impact on audiences and ticket sales. I do not feel the orchestra field can tolerate too many more shocks without some permanent erosion.

So much of the environment seems outside anyone's control. Ongoing conflict in the Middle East could degrade supply chains or cause an oil crisis. Our politics are the most intensely partisan environment since the Civil War, with the potential for domestic unrest high. Conflict in Gaza and Ukraine has already played a role in American politics; what if another international crisis erupts, this time in Asia or the Pacific? Or another major act of terrorism?

Throughout thirty years of raising money for orchestras, I learned that there are some folks who will give generously no matter what. There are many others who will only give generously, or at all, when they have strong confidence in their personal finances and feel they have provided for all their families' future needs. Domestic and international upheavals impacting the stock market can rock that confidence, creating a double whammy for non-profits: donors hesitant to give at a time when the value and earnings of existing endowments have gone through the floor.

SUMMARY: The willingness of many donors to give generously, or at all, is tied strongly to their own sense of personal wealth, which tracks largely to the stock market. Events outside our control may have a severe negative impact on the markets and other economic factors.

Culture War Issues

The orchestra field would seem to trend progressive, certainly if one looks at the statements, policies, and practices of its larger representatives and its advocacy organization. Mirroring this at the local level can be fraught, as we live in a world where everything is a partisan issue.

As a personal example, many began to use pronouns in correspondence and on meeting sites after the diversity reckoning of 2020. Not wanting to seem against this practice, I added "him/his" to my professional e-mail signature. I was then called on the carpet in a sponsorship meeting with a private funder, who said he was pretty sure he would fund my orchestra until he "saw all that 'they/them/he/she/it' business in your e-mail." Another funder expressed concern over the inclusion of a rainbow in an outdoor building mural associated with my organization, seeing that as "a political statement." Conversely, I have also faced the perception that because Mozart was a white man, his music is by extension only for white persons and that playing his music is somehow nothing but a promotion of the "patriarchy."

We are a divided country, and in this environment, it is my belief that arts organizations will face growing difficulty receiving public funding, as they find themselves trying to straddle a widening cultural gap. There was a brief bipartisan consensus about the role of public funding in the arts – for instance, the budget for the National Endowment for the Arts grew most rapidly under the Nixon administration. Now, in places where right-wing politics dominate, the arts run the risk of being deemed too "woke." As I write, the budget-cutting antics of "DOGE" are just getting underway. I will personally be pleasantly surprised if federal funding for the arts survives our current political moment.

In 2024, all general operating support grants to arts organizations in the state of Florida were reduced to zero, at a time that was not only without warning, but also within the fiscal year in question for most of those organizations. The reason? Allegedly "sexual" content within a Fringe theatre festival. That was enough for all non-capital support of the arts to go right out the window. I worried about my organization's budget with a six-figure grant from Florida's state arts agency; I would be even more worried without it.

There is always a place for creativity, innovation, and doing things differently, but after a time, I wonder if orchestras will be forced to change so radically that they either go out of business or become something unrecognizable from what we know today.

In places where left of center politics rule, the arts are in danger of being seen as too elite, too lacking in diversity, too associated with a narrow segment of society, too white, too affluent. As such, they are likely to fall in funders' favor relative to newer, more diverse organizations, ones which specifically "center" historically underserved populations. In the most benign manifestation, the funding pie will be sliced into smaller pieces. In a more hostile form, funding to traditional arts may be reduced or eliminated.

There was pressure on orchestras, at the time following the murder of George Floyd, to go full "woke" in light of a so-called "racial reckoning." Our service organization went so far as to say, in a creed-like statement, that we were in thrall to "white supremacy." Those times seem quite distant now, with the ascension of the second Trump administration, and I sympathize with orchestra leaders who must now feel batted about like a ping-pong ball during ongoing culture wars.
Challenges from the left, challenges from the right - fewer and fewer places are run with an ideology that would be deemed "moderate" or "centrist": in my view, the world view that is most likely to look with favor on the traditional performing arts.

Some have recommended that orchestras "take a stand" and become more politically active. This is, frankly, nonsense; first, it is contradictory to the non-profit model in which organizations receive at least some public funding and thus face strict limitations on lobbying or partisan activity. Second and more importantly, orchestras are governed by Boards that reflect a variety of political views. Orchestra's need for contributions from individuals with significant wealth guarantees that at least some of those Board members and significant donors will be politically conservative. It is madness to suggest that orchestras become overtly political; we must focus on art.

There is plenty of art that does make a political statement, and that is fine - orchestras have generally been able to weather some amount of resulting controversy, if, overall, they maintain an appearance of balance. In my career, I experienced older patrons – some World War II veterans – upset that a Japanese conductor was programming Penderecki's *Threnody to the Victims of Hiroshima*. My orchestra played it nonetheless, and most orchestras do a good job with overt patriotic performances as well, playing the service songs as a tribute to military service during outdoor concerts and the like. That is an example of good artistic balance. That is different from standing with one candidate or party. In my view, that is simply not the role of orchestras.

The challenge of our times is that almost everything has become political. Over thirty years managing orchestras, here are some of the other challenges I faced:
- During the Iraq War, playing the national anthem was interpreted as support for the war. Of course, NOT playing it was interpreted as failing to support the troops.
- Also during the Iraq War, an all-French program suddenly offended some; this was, of course, the "Freedom Fries" era.
- In 2014, an all-Russian program, planned months prior, quickly seemed tone-deaf as tanks rolled into Crimea. Conversely, in 2022, many organizations were quick to "stand with Ukraine" and make gestures of support toward that country, its artists, and its people. How this will be perceived going forward remains to be seen, now that our nation seems more sympathetic to the invader.
- A perennial challenge, outside the blue-state bubble, is LGBT issues. In my last position, I encountered a challenging situation when a venue affiliated with my orchestra presented a drag show

– more specifically, when a touring drag show it had presented for many years suddenly became controversial due to inflammatory coverage on Fox News.

The diversity issue is a real problem for orchestras. In some cases, it is a problem relative to the people served, the people in the audience, the people on the board, but in almost all cases, it is a problem relative to the people on stage, who generally do not mirror the demographics of the communities they serve.

There are many complicated reasons for this. In my view, they have a lot to do with class and the financial resources needed to pursue high level training in music. However, because there is a significant demographic overlap between class and race in our country, it easy to conflate the two and cast performing arts organizations as bastions of racism.

Orchestras can program Florence Price on every single concert if they wish, but they are still likely to have an appearance problem relative to the performers on stage for a long time, and relative, in many cases, to their histories, forever. This perception or reality will be a growing complication for orchestra's efforts to win support from funders both public and private. Complicating matters further, their efforts to correct this and prove a commitment to diversity may then attract the ire of conservative funders or perhaps even direct attack from government officials (see again, Florida state arts funding, 2024, and recent efforts by the federal government to eliminate all references to diversity, equity, and inclusion).

As the orchestra business model gets sixty percent of its revenue – or more – from contributions, I see many storm clouds on the horizon. Our base of support must be larger than the shrinking pool of true classical music aficionados, and our cause must be seen as broadly worthwhile across a wide swath of private, corporate, institutional and yes, governmental funders.

Maintaining such a perception in a world where everything quickly becomes politicized is going to be harder and harder. We cannot even agree on all working together in the face of natural disasters anymore – it is naïve to think that a majority will agree on the importance of the arts.

SUMMARY: In a time of great national division, orchestras are at constant risk of being caught in a culture war; too white, male, and traditional for the left, too "woke" for the right.

Future Public Health Emergencies

I saw four real "shocks to the system" during my career with orchestras: the recession of 1990 to 1991, 9/11, the financial collapse of 2008 to 2009, and the COVID-19 pandemic. The last two were by far the worst, and COVID will be the one with the most lasting impact. We hear a lot that "audiences have been slow to return from COVID" and it is my belief that a sizable portion never will. COVID was enough of a disruption, lasting for some orchestras for a full season or longer, that some folks changed their concertgoing habits for good.

This is the way in which the streaming era will be different from previous technological advents, including records, television, and the VCR, in that you have a new in-home entertainment option coming of age together with a disastrous pandemic during which those who could, just stayed home. The people able to stay home were the same people – older, more affluent, better educated – who comprise the bulk of our audiences. The result may be a permanent change in behavior affecting a good portion of the traditional core audience for the symphony.

Further, while welcome at the time, generous pandemic relief programs provided many orchestras with such an infusion of cash that their underlying financial challenges were masked, for a time, but are now coming back into full view, as they grapple with all the other issues I have mentioned.

Was COVID a once-in-a-century event, or will new transmissible diseases wreak more havoc in coming years? I fear the orchestra industry will not be able to face another bout of "everyone stay at home" anytime soon, if ever. Musicians playing in boxes on Zoom (or, in literal boxes, six feet apart on the stage) may have seemed novel and innovative at first, in the dark days of 2020. I do not see much appetite for a sequel.

What specially makes me shake my head is so much of what was emphasized in the early days of COVID is now known to have been unimportant. All those millions of gallons of hand sanitizer, the distancing, the plexiglass boxes around the trumpet player – all unhelpful, as silly in retrospect as those ridiculous elbow bumps in lieu of a handshake. It was about venue ventilation and masking all along. The complete failure of messaging and guidance around COVID has contributed to an environment where there is a notable lack of trust in public authorities of all kinds.

Our industry is about people coming together in common spaces, literal "mass gatherings." If we cannot do that, there is no reason to have the orchestra industry – any more than there was reason to have the New York Central Railroad once one could just take the highway.

SUMMARY: The COVID-19 pandemic was a shock to the orchestra system from which many are still recovering. If a similar pandemic occurs soon, it will be more than many organizations can survive.

Climate Change

I was on the site recently for the League of American Orchestras, and I noted they had a page for "Climate Change." I was quick to view it, thinking it might help shape some of my comments in this section. I found resources on reducing institutional "carbon footprint." While a long view is noble, I am afraid the problem may be much more immediate than installing solar panels and rooftop green space.

As I worked on this book I saw a monster hurricane barreling toward Florida, even as mountainous parts of Tennessee, Georgia, and the Carolinas were reeling from unprecedented flooding from a previous storm. I saw much of Los Angeles being evacuated due to out-of-control wildfires, with a real, specific impact on our industry; musicians' and patrons' homes lost in neighborhoods burned to the ground, the rental library for the music of Arnold Schonberg reduced to cinders.

To put it bluntly, if these kinds of catastrophic weather disruptions become more common, and more violent – and there is a scientific consensus that they will – it will be hard to focus a great deal of attention on opening night for the local symphony orchestra.

In fairness, the League's site does have a separate page for "Disaster Relief and Preparedness."

The big issue is this: organized classical music events can objectively be said to fall at the top of pyramid for Maslow's hierarchy of needs – aligning with "self-actualization" and "esteem." The point of that hierarchy is to point out how the upper tiers of the pyramid may be reached only when the first two tiers – physiological needs like food and shelter, security needs like employment and health care – are firmly in place. When life may regularly be disrupted by catastrophic events, and resources are urgently needed to address disasters, it will be harder to ask people to prioritize ticket purchases and funders to prioritize donations to the arts.

Even when events are merely postponed, regular postponements and cancellations of concerts due to extreme weather events are bound to further erode the already declining audience for the traditional, fixed-seat subscription. Like it or not, the field has yet to find a truly workable replacement, by which I mean one that works not only for the audience but also generates the revenue orchestras have come to expect from subscriptions.

It is not just hurricanes for the mid-Atlantic and southeast and the wildfires in California. We will also confront an increased risk of tornadoes in the midwest, scorching heat in the southwest, and greater flooding risks almost everywhere. To once again make it very specific to our field, the past decades have seen multiple orchestra concert halls inundated by what were characterized as "500-year" or "1,000-year" floods.

All of these events are potentially disruptive to orchestras trying to offer a regular series of concerts, hand in hand with regular employment for musicians. I hope I am being an alarmist, but remember, Diamond's theory of collapse is that it comes about through a combination of factors, not through one factor alone.

SUMMARY: An increasing number of extreme weather events will disrupt daily life in an increasing number of places, increasingly often. At the least, this will make concert schedules unreliable, weakening confidence in subscriptions and other advance ticket purchases. At the worst, arts attendance will no longer be a priority due to its upward placement in Maslow's hierarchy.

Internal Strife

A recent ugly scandal at the New York Philharmonic has received a great deal of publicity. Two musicians were accused of assaulting another in 2010. No action was taken for several years, then, in 2018, after the rise of the "#MeToo" movement, the two alleged offenders were dismissed. The musicians' union filed a grievance, and "binding arbitration" resulted in their reinstatement in 2020. After an article was published exploring the situation, they were suspended once again. This situation will certainly get settled out of court, in a manner that will cost a good deal of money. The damage to the orchestra's reputation – and to that of the field as a whole – will be hard to quantify but could be equally costly. The New York Phil is not the only orchestra, unfortunately, which has had a public reckoning with these sorts of issues.

Meanwhile, in San Antonio, a complex imbroglio developed in which two rival boards are suing each other for control of a successor organization begun by the orchestra's musicians after the predecessor went out of business. Complicating matters further, a rival orchestra with a different business model arrived on the scene and usurped the first orchestra's place in the region's premier performing arts center. All this internecine warfare is occurring in the context of an orchestra with a long history of turmoil and financial issues. This sort of internal conflict is the last thing needed by an organization that, one would think, should be trying to regain the confidence of donors and the public. These are just two examples of the final threat I see to the field: internecine warfare, usually over financial issues, but increasingly over workplace culture problems as well. The orchestra field faces many challenges, but oftentimes, as it goes in horror movies, the calls are coming from inside the house.

Make no mistake, when there have been egregious internal

problems with such things as harassment and racism, they must be corrected, but when an organization has these issues play out in a public way, there is potential for loss of public confidence and erosion of funder support. With time and leadership imbued with moral clarity, it may be restored. Unfortunately, public fighting between constituents of an orchestra, no matter how justified or necessary, often plays out in a chaotic manner good only for headline writers.

There is never a good time for such challenges, but I worry that this unique moment – a time of great national division, of ongoing uncertainty in the aftermath of COVID, of international unrest, of increasing funder skepticism – is perhaps the worst possible time for an orchestra to appear, publicly, as the proverbial circular firing squad.

SUMMARY: Some orchestras are dealing with formerly hidden internal conflicts and injustices in a very public way. There is also constant labor-management tension in the field, which means organizations may be facing challenging external issues without internal alignment.

If you have read this far, you are no doubt thinking, "Wow, this guy is GLOOMY." I do not mean to spark depression; rather, I am simply trying to provide a realistic assessment of potential challenges. The field has challenges, and it has problems, and it is foolish not to acknowledge them as such.

I have always been the person who would prefer to be wrong about a potential negative than a potential positive. To use an automotive metaphor, I fill up long before I get to a quarter of a tank; I never assume there will be a convenient gas station once the little "E" has come on.

There are plenty of places you can go for rah-rah "happy talk." Instead, I want to point out that as tough as things have been in the past, they are likely to get tougher. That means we must get our act together.

I do believe that orchestras will survive – just not all of them. Only orchestras with skillful leadership and strong internal alignment will weather tough times successfully. Whether yours will be one that makes it depends in large part on the choices you make, in understanding your organization, its strengths and weaknesses, and how you choose to address them.

It is not about quick fixes, new slogans, or messianic leadership. It is not about rushing to follow the political moment; as we see, that can change like the wind. It is about working together, as a team, with everyone understanding their roles and doing what they do for the love of music and community. That is the only sustainable path to the future.

Internal alignment occurs when all constituencies understand and respect one another. That is where it must all begin. It is my hope the information I have presented here will be helpful in promoting that understanding.

ABOUT THE AUTHOR

Paul A. Helfrich

Paul A. Helfrich began his orchestral career as Director of Marketing & Public Relations with the Kalamazoo Symphony Orchestra in 1990. Over the course of a 33-year career with American orchestras, he went on to serve as Executive Director with the Erie Philharmonic, West Virginia Symphony, Dayton Philharmonic, and Orlando Philharmonic. He played a key role in the formation of the Dayton Performing Arts Alliance, a first-of-its-kind merger of opera, ballet, and orchestra, and served the organization as its first President & CEO.

In other professional activities, Mr. Helfrich served as Chairman of Manager's Meeting Group 3 for the League of American Orchestras and as a Grant Panelist for the Florida Division of Arts & Culture, Cuyahoga Arts & Culture, and the Pennsylvania Council on the Arts.

Mr. Helfrich resides in Raleigh, North Carolina with his wife, the violinist Jessica Hung, and in retirement has devoted himself to painting and playing the electric bass. This is his first book.

www.ingramcontent.com/pod-product-compliance
Lightning Source LLC
Chambersburg PA
CBHW050917160426
43194CB00011B/2438